The

OHIO KNITTING MILLS

KNITTING BOOK

The OHIO KNITTING MILLS

KNITTING BOOK

STEVEN TATAR *with* **DENISE GROLLMUS**

Fashion Photography by ANNA WOLF

Artisan
NEW YORK

Published by Artisan
A Division of Workman Publishing Company, Inc.
225 Varick Street
New York, NY 10014-4381
www.artisanbooks.com

Library of Congress Cataloging-in-Publication Data
Tatar, Steven.
The Ohio Knitting Mills knitting book / Steven Tatar with Denise Grollmus.
    p. cm.
ISBN 978-1-57965-399-6
1. Knitting—Patterns. 2. Ohio Knitting Mills. I. Grollmus, Denise. II. Title.
TT825.T342 2010
746.43'2—dc22   2009038949

Design by Susan E. Baldaserini
Patterns adapted and written by Alexandra Virgiel

Printed in China
First printing, July 2010

1 3 5 7 9 10 8 6 4 2

Previous spread: *A Raschel knitting machine on the floor at Stone*
Knitting Mills, the precursor to Ohio Knitting Mills, c. 1930.

TO OUR GRANDFATHERS

—S.T.

CONTENTS

Opposite: *Christmas dinner for the Cutting Department, 1933. Harry Stone sits front and center.*

The OHIO KNITTING MILLS

KNITTING BOOK

Opposite: *Ohio Knitting Mills workers standing in front of a Raschel warp knitting machine, c. 1949. Tom Rovas, OKM's knitting engineer (see page 31), stands at the far left.*

THE STORY OF THE OHIO KNITTING MILLS

What makes the sweaters in this book so alluring, aside from their quirky vibrancy and vintage appeal, is the history they all share—a tale that begins in the mid-1920s, in Cleveland, Ohio, with two men who had little more than five hundred dollars, a car, and a big dream.

Throughout the early 1920s, Harry Stone had worked his way up from a floor sweeper to head salesman at the Rich-Sampliner Knitting Mills Co. in Cleveland, Ohio. At the time, Cleveland was one of the nation's largest apparel manufacturing centers, along with Philadelphia and New York City. Cleveland's East Side was crowded with large brick factories, which housed a wide range of industries, including textile

manufacturers that busily churned out everything from bedsheets to designer dresses.

In those early days of American fashion, a talented salesman could make or break a collection. Harry had earned himself a reputation for being one of Cleveland's best salesmen as well as a charismatic carouser. His bulky frame, always clad in tailored suits, displayed his insatiable appetite for life. After work, he retired to the bars, which buzzed with epic tales of his antics. A favorite story was the time he showed up at New York's Hotel Pennsylvania—immortalized in Glenn Miller's song "Pennsylvania 6-5000"—to meet with the wholesale buyers for Sears, Roebuck. He'd arrive with

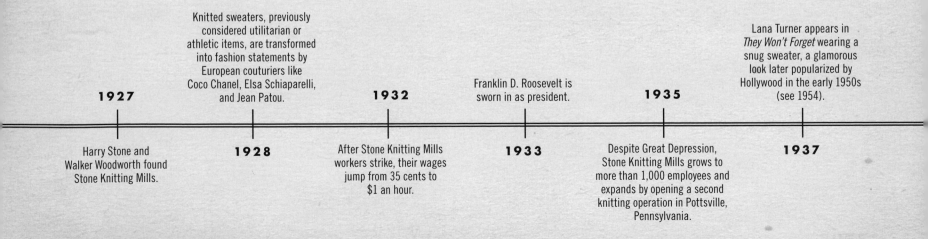

1927

Harry Stone and Walker Woodworth found Stone Knitting Mills.

Knitted sweaters, previously considered utilitarian or athletic items, are transformed into fashion statements by European couturiers like Coco Chanel, Elsa Schiaparelli, and Jean Patou.

1928

1932

After Stone Knitting Mills workers strike, their wages jump from 35 cents to $1 an hour.

Franklin D. Roosevelt is sworn in as president.

1933

1935

Despite Great Depression, Stone Knitting Mills grows to more than 1,000 employees and expands by opening a second knitting operation in Pottsville, Pennsylvania.

Lana Turner appears in *They Won't Forget* wearing a snug sweater, a glamorous look later popularized by Hollywood in the early 1950s (see 1954).

1937

three suitcases, promising to show his customers the best of Sampliner's fall line. As he made his announcement, his assistant opened a suitcase stocked not with sweaters but with bottles of booze. "I told you it was the best line we ever made," Harry joked.

By 1925, business had turned sour for Sampliner. The company's sales fell so dramatically that it decided to liquidate its assets and close up shop. Rather than feel doomed by the loss of his job, Harry seized the moment as a great opportunity. He could finally fulfill his lifelong dream of being his own boss.

He partnered with an equally driven man, Walker Woodworth, who'd been Sampliner's plant manufacturing supervisor. The pair couldn't have been more opposite—where Harry had a talent for entertaining, Walker was stern and serious—but this led to a logical division of labor. Walker would be the inside man, supervising the plant, and Harry would be in charge of sales, wining and dining customers as the face of the company. They pooled their resources—little

more than the sum of Walker's car and Harry's five hundred dollars' worth of savings—and incorporated Stone Knitting Mills in 1927.

The men opened up shop in the National Screw building, a massive factory that housed a number of manufacturing outfits, located on Stanton Avenue in the heart of Cleveland's East Side district. It was an area bustling with industry and a colorful collection of ethnic groups who scoured the local businesses for work. Stone Knitting occupied a portion of the first few floors of the building, where it made men's pullovers, cardigans, and shirts on roughly a dozen knitting machines.

By 1930, as the full impact of the Great Depression hit the United States, almost half of the textile and knitting mills in Cleveland had already gone out of business. Not Stone Knitting. Thanks to Walker's intense work ethic and Harry's contagious moxie, the Mills was working overtime to supply the nation with beautifully made knitwear. Every day, unemployed workers collected outside the National Screw building hoping to find a job on Stone's factory floor.

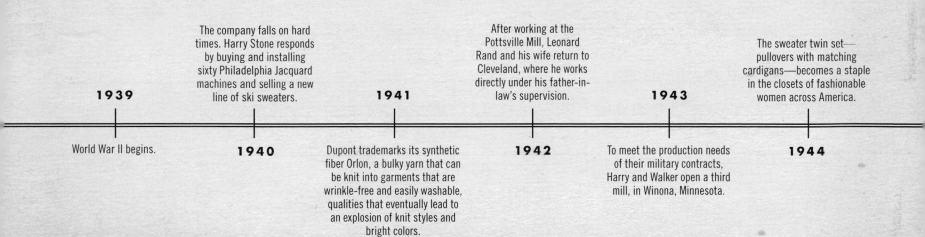

1939

World War II begins.

The company falls on hard times. Harry Stone responds by buying and installing sixty Philadelphia Jacquard machines and selling a new line of ski sweaters.

1940

Dupont trademarks its synthetic fiber Orlon, a bulky yarn that can be knit into garments that are wrinkle-free and easily washable, qualities that eventually lead to an explosion of knit styles and bright colors.

1941

After working at the Pottsville Mill, Leonard Rand and his wife return to Cleveland, where he works directly under his father-in-law's supervision.

1942

To meet the production needs of their military contracts, Harry and Walker open a third mill, in Winona, Minnesota.

1943

The sweater twin set— pullovers with matching cardigans—becomes a staple in the closets of fashionable women across America.

1944

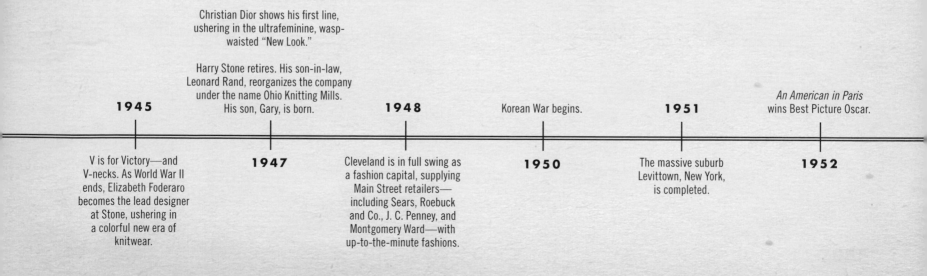

The National Screw & Jack Company.

When it was established in 1927, Stone Knitting Mills' first home was the National Screw and Tack Company building. This massive structure was one of many industrial complexes in Cleveland then housing a myriad of manufacturing concerns.

The company earned a reputation for treating its employees well. On every major holiday, Harry would organize a huge party, lavishing workers with a hearty meal and dancing. Theresa Yacabucci, who was hired at Stone in 1930 at the tender age of seventeen, described the mill as her home away from home, her second family. By the time Franklin D. Roosevelt was sworn into office in 1933, she was making one dollar an hour in the trimming department, where she remained for the next sixty years, until she retired.

By 1935, the company had more than one thousand employees at its Cleveland plant. These workers ran the various knitting, cutting, and sewing machines that produced everything from men's snowflake-dotted ski sweaters and sleek poor boy shirts to novelty fabrics like brushed mohair looks and faux fur pieces for women. Meanwhile, Harry and Walker were growing their business, opening up a second plant, in Pottsville, Pennsylvania.

But as many rag-trade men had learned, fashion is a fickle business. By 1940, the company had fallen on hard times. Tastes were changing and knitting techniques along with them. Harry responded by purchasing sixty Philadelphia

---

Christian Dior shows his first line, ushering in the ultrafeminine, waspwaisted "New Look."

Harry Stone retires. His son-in-law, Leonard Rand, reorganizes the company under the name Ohio Knitting Mills. His son, Gary, is born.

1945

1947

1948

Korean War begins.

1951

An American in Paris wins Best Picture Oscar.

V is for Victory—and V-necks. As World War II ends, Elizabeth Foderaro becomes the lead designer at Stone, ushering in a colorful new era of knitwear.

Cleveland is in full swing as a fashion capital, supplying Main Street retailers— including Sears, Roebuck and Co., J. C. Penney, and Montgomery Ward—with up-to-the-minute fashions.

1950

The massive suburb Levittown, New York, is completed.

1952

Jacquard machines, a huge risk considering they didn't even have samples from these machines to show prospective customers. That didn't seem to worry Harry, who quickly bought up samples made by other mills and used them to drum up business. Before the machines were even delivered to the factory, he had already sold the entire line of new jacquard styles, from men's cardigans to women's twin sets, and the Mills was soon pumping out sweaters three shifts a day.

A year later, once America entered World War II, equipping the armed forces became a top national priority for the country's manufacturers. Stone amassed numerous military contracts and opend a third facility, the Winona Knitting Mills in Minnesota. Soon its three different plants were producing a range of critical war supplies, from camouflage material to watch caps for the troops. Meanwhile, the factory floors swelled with an influx of women who entered the workforce to help with the war effort.

As the war drew to an end, both Harry and Walker were considering retirement. After nearly twenty years of building and running their business, the two men decided it was time to hand over the reins to a new generation. While Walker's son, Leslie, would take over the Winona Mills in Minnesota, Harry's son-in-law, Leonard Rand, who had been running the Pottsville operation, was brought back to Ohio and groomed to lead the main factory in Cleveland.

Before marrying into the Stone family, Leonard had had no experience in the fashion industry. He was an ascetic man who had studied actuarial science and preferred the paperwork of his office to his father-in-law's leisurely business meetings. Still, Harry could see that Leonard and the Mills would be a perfect match. Leonard's gift for crunching numbers would benefit the company's profit margin, and his tireless work ethic and keen eye for anticipating trends would keep the Mills on top of the knitwear game. In spite of his

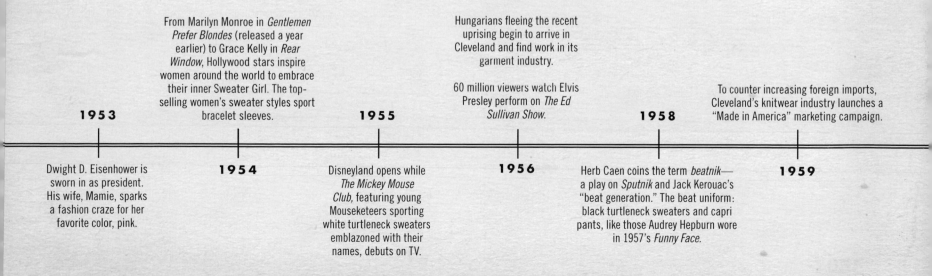

From Marilyn Monroe in *Gentlemen Prefer Blondes* (released a year earlier) to Grace Kelly in *Rear Window*, Hollywood stars inspire women around the world to embrace their inner Sweater Girl. The top-selling women's sweater styles sport bracelet sleeves.

Hungarians fleeing the recent uprising begin to arrive in Cleveland and find work in its garment industry.

60 million viewers watch Elvis Presley perform on *The Ed Sullivan Show.*

To counter increasing foreign imports, Cleveland's knitwear industry launches a "Made in America" marketing campaign.

1953

1955

1958

Dwight D. Eisenhower is sworn in as president. His wife, Mamie, sparks a fashion craze for her favorite color, pink.

1954

Disneyland opens while *The Mickey Mouse Club,* featuring young Mouseketeers sporting white turtleneck sweaters emblazoned with their names, debuts on TV.

1956

Herb Caen coins the term *beatnik*— a play on *Sputnik* and Jack Kerouac's "beat generation." The beat uniform: black turtleneck sweaters and capri pants, like those Audrey Hepburn wore in 1957's *Funny Face.*

1959

Even as early as 1951, Leonard's associates at a Cleveland meeting of the National Knitted Outerwear Association expressed deep concern for the increasing number of goods coming in from Asia. The company tried everything, from launching a "Made in America" campaign to asking congressmen to restrict the number of imports, but ultimately, they could not hold off these changes. From 1950 to 1980, the number of knitting mills in Cleveland dropped from more than twenty-five to fewer than ten.

Yet the Ohio Knitting Mills managed to stay afloat much longer than most of its counterparts, thanks to Leonard's gift for squeezing the most profit out of a pound of yarn. But even his genius couldn't save the company from the sad fate of American manufacturing as a whole. By the time Leonard's son, Gary, was getting ready to take over the Mills at the turn of the century, almost all of the company's business had already fled overseas. Even the few fashion labels that had remained fiercely loyal to OKM, like Pendleton Woolen Mills of Oregon and Liz Claiborne, couldn't resist the much cheaper production costs of Asian vendors.

Still, the designs coming off the Ohio Knitting Mills' Raschel knitting machines were truly distinctive and unparalleled. For this reason, throughout the 1990s, high-end labels like Ralph Lauren would continue to come to OKM to have their sample lines produced. Though this gesture may have been flattering, it wasn't enough to keep the company in business—the samples would then be sent to Asia, where another manufacturer would copy the Mills' work, at a much lower price.

In 2001 Leonard died after a stroke. A year later, OKM received a letter from Pendleton, saying that it would no longer be doing business with the Ohio Knitting Mills. OKM's last major customer was shifting to lower-cost overseas production. Leonard's son, Gary, now president of the company,

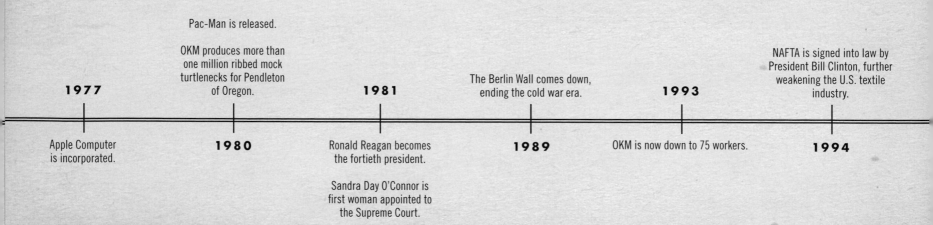

Pac-Man is released.

OKM produces more than one million ribbed mock turtlenecks for Pendleton of Oregon.

NAFTA is signed into law by President Bill Clinton, further weakening the U.S. textile industry.

The Berlin Wall comes down, ending the cold war era.

1977　　**1981**　　**1993**

Apple Computer is incorporated.

1980

Ronald Reagan becomes the fortieth president.

1989

OKM is now down to 75 workers.

1994

Sandra Day O'Connor is first woman appointed to the Supreme Court.

Dozens of seamstresses at the Mills cut and sewed the knit fabrics into finished garments (c. 1950s).

That's when I happened to wander through Gary's doors and into another time. The company had saved its massive archive of knitwear, from the 1920s poor boy shirts to the Mr. Cleaver cardigans of the '50s and the disco-ready dresses of the '70s. While the storeroom seemed like little more than clutter from the closing mills, I saw the opportunity for an entirely new brand of vintage-inspired, forward-looking clothing—wearable pieces of history, reknit in today's colors and yarns. And so a new chapter of the Ohio Knitting Mills was opened.

This book is an invitation to this new era of the Ohio Knitting Mills—a celebration not only of the company and four decades of sportswear fashion, but also of American creativity and style.

sold the OKM building to the City of Cleveland. He also sold off the equipment, knitting machines, and thousands of tons of yarn to various buyers.

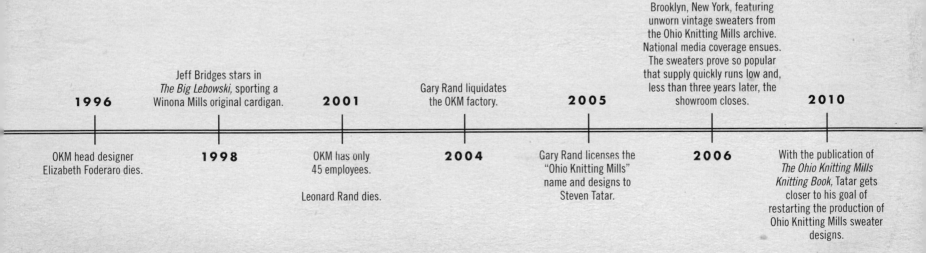

1996
OKM head designer Elizabeth Foderaro dies.

1998

Jeff Bridges stars in *The Big Lebowski*, sporting a Winona Mills original cardigan.

2001
OKM has only 45 employees.

Leonard Rand dies.

2004

Gary Rand liquidates the OKM factory.

2005
Gary Rand licenses the "Ohio Knitting Mills" name and designs to Steven Tatar.

Tatar opens a showroom in Brooklyn, New York, featuring unworn vintage sweaters from the Ohio Knitting Mills archive. National media coverage ensues. The sweaters prove so popular that supply quickly runs low and, less than three years later, the showroom closes.

2006

2010
With the publication of *The Ohio Knitting Mills Knitting Book*, Tatar gets closer to his goal of restarting the production of Ohio Knitting Mills sweater designs.

ABBREVIATIONS

beg	beginning		**rem**	remain, remaining
CC	contrast color		**rep**	repeat
cn	cable needle		**rnd**	round
dec	decrease, decreased		**RS**	right side
dpn	double-pointed needle(s)			(front-facing side
est	established			of a garment)
foll	following, follows		**sl**	slip
inc	increase, increased		**ssk**	slip, slip knit
k	knit			decrease
m1	make 1 stitch		**st**	stitch
MC	main color		**St st**	Stockinette stitch
p	purl		**tbl**	through back loop
p2sso	pass 2 slipped stitches over		**tog**	together
patt	pattern		**WS**	wrong side
pm	place marker		**yo**	yarn over

Note: Finished length measurements are taken from the top of the back neck to the hem unless otherwise noted. Because of the sloping shape of the shoulders in most patterns, the finished length measurement will not always match the hem-to-outside-shoulder measurement.

Opposite: Downtown Cleveland, looking from the west over the Flats, the city's original industrial zone along the Cuyahoga River, c. 1954.

PROJECTS IN THIS CHAPTER

The 1940s

THE BIRTH OF SPORTSWEAR

By 1947 America was adjusting to postwar life. Men had returned from the war and reentered the workforce, while women moved out of the workforce to reembrace their roles as wives, mothers, and homemakers. The American "industrial war machine" had redirected its considerable output from tanks and fighter planes to consumer goods, and the GI Bill offered people easy credit to readily partake of the new bounty. Across the land, folks exuberantly embraced a lifestyle that emphasized mobility, convenience, and leisure. The baby boom was also in full swing as the country happily put World War II and a decade of economic depression behind it.

This was also the year that Leonard Rand assumed management of the Stone Knitting Mills. Up until Rand took over, the Mills had produced mostly men's knitwear—from cardigans and pullovers to their famous Poor Boy shirts. During the war, the company largely relied on military contracts for business, producing millions of Navy watchman sweaters and acres of camouflage fabric for the armed forces.

As Rand was reorganizing his father-in-law's business into the Ohio Knitting Mills, America was experiencing a cultural rebirth. Weary of the forced modesty and drab grays and browns that described much of fashion from the Great Depression through World War II, consumers now yearned for a vibrant array of clothing that would reflect their new optimism for a bright future.

As men shed their military uniforms and women stepped out of factory coveralls, the Ohio Knitting Mills delivered knitwear that matched the country's new tastes—from lively pieces for the new workingman to a new line for women. Across the fashion spectrum, women's silhouettes grew sexier, the color schemes more vivacious, and the selection more diverse.

The sweaters in this chapter—selected from the archives of both the Stone and Ohio Knitting Mills—also reflect a crucial transition in twentieth-century American culture and fashion: the emergence of sportswear. Where the fashion industry had long been dominated by high-end European designers and a more formal sense of dressing, style was now being driven by family-owned, American-based companies like Stone Knitting Mills, which were set on creating comfortable, functional, and affordable clothing for both work and play.

In the postwar era, sportswear became as synonymous with what it meant to be American as baseball and apple pie. Its popularity reflected the mobility and practicality of contemporary life, as well as the newfound prosperity of the middle class.

OHIO KNITTING MILLS

Original Design

Fall   19 47

4701 PERKINS AVENUE
CLEVELAND, O. 44103

New American Gentleman

World War II was in full swing. More than ten million of America's men were off fighting in Europe and the Pacific theater, while women entered the workforce in droves—hundreds of thousands of Rosie the Riveters doing their part to support the war effort. And some found a home at Stone Knitting Mills.

During the war, Stone employed more than 1,300 workers—mostly women—at its Cleveland plant, located in the massive National Screw building. Here, amid the cacophony of streetcars and manufacturing, hordes of European immigrants and African American transplants from the South came in search of the American Dream. The area was a patchwork of ethnicity and imposing brick buildings, housing everything from textile mills to lightbulb makers, delis, and twenty-four-hour bars for the multitude of workers filling up three shifts a day.

Stone Knitting Mills churned out more than two million sweaters specifically for the troops. Employees claimed that by the war's end, they could no longer bear the sight of khaki. The same went for veterans returning from the front—a fact well understood by Stone.

The New American Gentleman was certainly designed with the postwar man in mind. It was not only a breath of fresh air after the tired military palette, but also a vibrant expression of the optimism and vast opportunities of the postwar era. In addition, it was meant to be an extremely versatile piece for the workingman of all seasons, whether as a stylish statement over a shirt and tie in the spring, or an insulating accent under a winter wool suit.

Still, the canary yellow and tangerine orange of this piece would not have been possible without the war that folks were so earnestly putting behind them. As raw materials such as wool and natural pigments became scarce during the early 1940s, military researchers began playing with textile and dye technology, creating synthetic fabrics as well as a whole new palette of ersatz pigments. Soon, retailers realized the potential of such inventions—usurping them for use in their own products and then marketing them as "modern" and "improved," thus translating a utilitarian design into an immediate fashion trend.

Sixty years later, the bright color scheme of this vest is incredibly fresh. It can be easily reinterpreted as hip-hop preppy or tongue-in-cheek geek chic. The real beauty, however, is that you can be just as inventive as its creators by choosing your own palette of unusual hues.

This project is appropriate for a knitter with moderate to advanced skills. We redrew the chest embroidery pattern as a modified argyle design; or try your own 1940s-inspired design!

SIZES
Men's S (M, L, XL)

FINISHED MEASUREMENTS
Chest 34 (38, 42, 46) inches
Length 23½ (24, 25, 25½) inches

YARNS
Filatura di Crosa Zara (100% merino wool; 136 yds per 50 g)
MC: #1424 Midnight Blue, 4 (5, 6, 7) skeins
CC: #1494 Light Gray, 3 (3, 4, 5) skeins

Tahki Cotton Classic (100% mercerized cotton; 105 yds per 50 g)
A: #3997 Bright Red, 1 skein
B: #3723 Light Lime Green, 1 skein

NEEDLES
U.S. size 5 (3.75 mm) circular needle, 24 inches long
U.S. size 4 (3.5 mm) straight needles
Adjust needle sizes as needed to obtain gauge.

NOTIONS
One U.S. size 10 (6 mm) straight needle
Stitch holder
Tapestry needle
Stitch marker
Dressmaker's tracing transfer paper

GAUGE
24 sts and 34 rows = 4 inches/10 cm in St st on circular needle

STITCH INSTRUCTIONS
Crossed Stitch
Row 1 (WS): With A or B and U.S. size 10 needle, purl.
Row 2 (RS): With A or B and the circular needle, *lift the second st on the left needle over the first and knit it, then knit the first st; rep from * to end.
Row 3 (RS): Do not turn work. Slide knitting down to other end of circular needle and work another RS row as follows: With MC or CC and the circular needle, k1, *lift the second st on the left needle over the first and knit it, then knit the first st; rep from * to last st, k1.

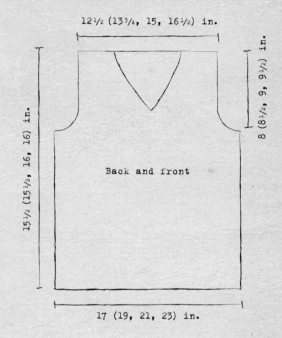

12½ (13¾, 15, 16½) in.

8 (8½, 9, 9½) in.

15½ (15½, 16, 16) in.

Back and front

17 (19, 21, 23) in.

BACK

With straight needles and MC, cast on 104 (116, 128, 140) sts. Work k1, p1 rib for 3 inches. Change to circular needle and continue in St st until piece measures 15½ (15½, 16, 16) inches from cast-on edge, ending with a WS row.

Shape Armholes

Bind off 6 sts at beg of next 2 rows. Bind off 4 sts at beg of next 2 rows. Bind off 3 sts at beg of next 2 rows—78 (90, 102, 114) sts rem.

Dec row (RS): k1, ssk, k to last 3 sts, k2tog, k1.

Rep Dec row on every following RS row until 74 (82, 90, 98) sts rem.

Work even until armholes measure 8 (8½, 9, 9½) inches. Bind off.

FRONT

With straight needles and CC, cast on 104 (116, 128, 140) sts. Work k1, p1 rib for 3 inches. Change to circular needle and continue in St st until piece measures 13 (13, 13½, 13½) inches from cast-on edge, ending with a RS row.

Work 3 rows Crossed Stitch patt with A, then MC.

Work 4 rows in St st with MC.

Work 3 rows Crossed Stitch patt with B, then MC.

Work 30 rows in St st with MC.

Work 3 rows Crossed Stitch patt with B, then MC.

Work 4 rows in St st with MC.

Work 3 rows Crossed Stitch patt with A, then CC.

Continue in St st with CC for remainder of Front.

AT THE SAME TIME, when piece measures 15½ (15½, 16, 16) inches from cast-on edge, shape armholes as for Back. When armhole shaping is complete, shape V-neck as follows:

Row 1 (RS): Work 37 (41, 45, 49) sts in patt and turn; place rem sts on holder.

Row 2 (WS): Work even.

Row 3: Work to last 3 sts, k2tog, k1.

Rep Rows 2 and 3 until 16 (18, 22, 24) sts rem.

Work even until armhole measures same as Back to shoulder. Bind off.

Join yarn to rem 37 (41, 45, 49) sts with RS facing.

Row 1 (RS): Work sts in patt to end.

Row 2 (WS): Work even.

Row 3: k1, ssk, work to end.

Rep Rows 2 and 3 until 16 (18, 22, 24) sts rem.

Work even until armhole measures same as Back to shoulder. Bind off.

FINISHING

Join right shoulder seam.

Neckband

With MC, straight needles, and RS facing, beg at left front shoulder, pick up and knit 3 sts for every 4 rows down left neck edge (taking care to end up with an even number of sts), 1 st at center front neck, 3 sts for every 4 rows up right neck edge, and 1 st in every bound-off st along back neck. Adjust as necessary to make total stitch count a multiple of 2 sts. Mark single center front st.

Row 1 (WS): *p1, k1; rep from * to center front st, p marked st, *k1, p1; rep from * to last st, k1.

Row 2 (RS): Work in k1, p1 rib as established to 1 st before center front st, sl2, k1, p2sso, replace marker in st just made, continue in est rib to end.

Row 3: Work in est rib to center front st, p marked st, rib to end.

Rep Rows 2 and 3 until neckband measures ¾ (¾, 1, 1) inch. Bind off in rib.

Join left shoulder and neckband seam.

Armhole Edgings

With MC, straight needles, and RS facing, beg at underarm, pick up and knit 1 st in every bound-off st and 3 sts for every 4 rows around armhole, ending up with an even number of sts. Work k1, p1 rib for ¾ (¾, 1, 1) inch. Bind off in rib.

Sew side and armhole edging seams. Weave in ends. Block.

Embroidery

Prepare the Template

Using a photocopy machine and the diamond embroidery template on page 18, enlarge the image so that the height of the diamond fits into the large blue band on the sweater's chest. A copy shop can assist you.

Transfer the Template

Note: Be sure to use dressmaker's tracing paper in a shade that will show up on the knitted fabric.

Lay the sweater on a hard surface. Center the template in the middle of the dark blue band just below the V-neck shaping (refer to the photo on page 14). Place the tracing paper beneath the template and pin through both layers to attach them to the sweater. Using a ballpoint pen, trace right on top of the diamond design, pressing so that the design transfers to the sweater. When you are finished, the design should be legible on the sweater.

Repeat the process across the entire chest panel, matching up the diamond designs. At the underarms, there will be only part of the diamond design (see Embroidery Guide).

Embroider Pattern

Note: Use a single strand of yarn throughout.

Using A, work the diamond motif in Outline st (see photo on page 14). Using B, work the smaller diamond motifs in Outline st.

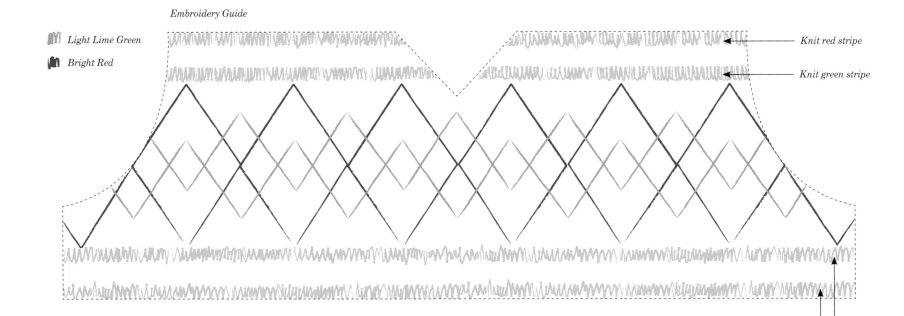

Embroidery Guide

〰 *Light Lime Green*

〰 *Bright Red*

Knit red stripe

Knit green stripe

Knit red stripe

Knit green stripe

CLEVELAND: AMERICA'S FASHION CAPITAL

In 1947, the *Davison's Knit Goods Trade* annual listed over twenty-three pages of dyers, spinners, sewers, knitting mills, garment makers, button suppliers, and zipper manufacturers in Cleveland alone. In fact, the city was one of the nation's largest apparel manufacturing centers, along with Philadelphia and New York.

In the first half of the twentieth century, the city's East Side was a bustling mecca of garment production, where shirts, dresses, suits, overcoats, hosiery, and especially knitwear were created. These factories housed manufacturers like Ohio Knitting Mills, Lion Knitting, and Majestic Knitwear, who supplied finished goods to hundreds of labels nationally, including some who called Cleveland home, such as Bobbie Brooks, Campus Casuals, Dalton, and Lampl.

During the Great Depression, folks desperate for work would often find a job in the city's vast garment district, which was central to supplying Main Street America with a significant portion of its outerwear, everything from men's jackets to women's overcoats to knit sweaters. They were sold through Chicago-based Sears, Roebuck and Co.—the world's largest retailer during this period—and through such competitors as Montgomery Ward, J. C. Penney, and Spiegel, as well as hundreds of smaller stores. It was Midwestern manufacturers—not the high-end designers in New York, Paris, or Milan—who determined what the majority of Americans wore.

By the late 1960s Cleveland's clothing industry had begun to decline. A complex set of circumstances—changing international tariff laws, new environmental legislation, the explosion of cheap imports from overseas manufacturers, and the emergence of big-box retailers whom they supplied—conspired to eventually make American apparel manufacturing a thing of the past.

Leonard Rand appearing on the local NBC affiliate, late 1940s.

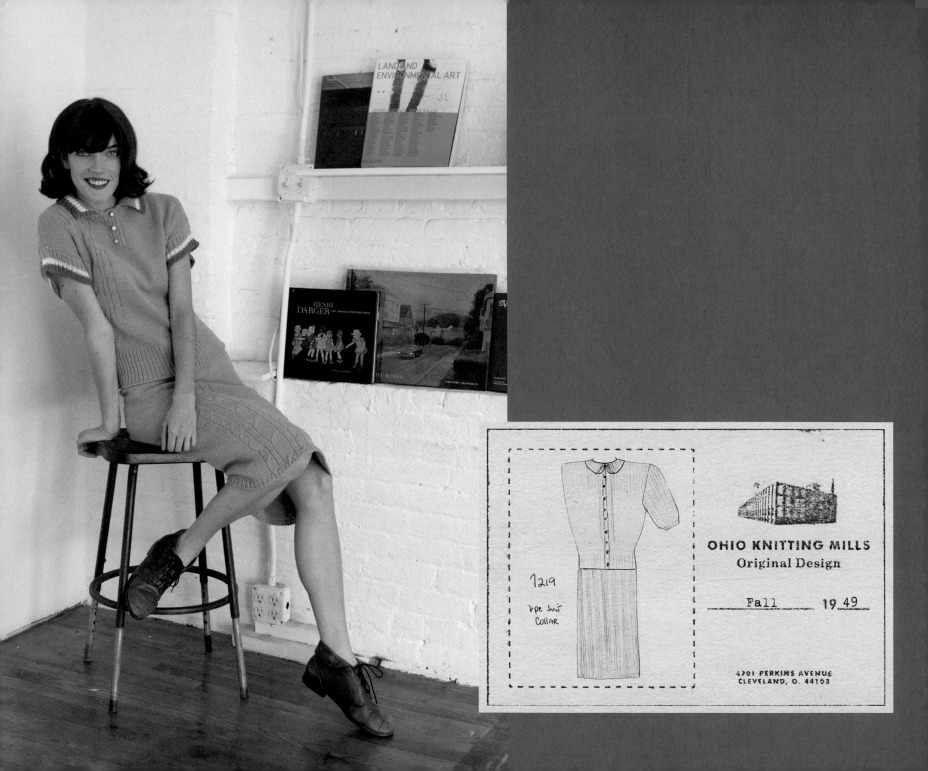

OHIO KNITTING MILLS

Original Design

7219

rpe suit
Collar

Fall ___ 19 49

4701 PERKINS AVENUE
CLEVELAND, O. 44103

Le Petit Pull et Amie

As American men expanded their wardrobes to include more casual wear, women were also making room in their closets for more playful pieces. Tired of the boxy, military styles that defined ladies' fashion during the ration-restricted war years, women welcomed clothing that celebrated a new femininity, defined by form-flattering shapes such as those inspired by Christian Dior's "New Look."

By the late 1940s, women were experimenting with separates—skirts as well as slacks—paired with a variety of tops. As their upwardly mobile lifestyles required more flexible wardrobes, knits proved to be particularly well suited for traditional pieces that were modest enough for the morality of the era, but still allowed women to move freely. Knitwear also provided an endless offering of decorative possibilities, delivering both style and comfort all in one coordinate.

While Stone Knitting Mills had largely focused on menswear, by the time it was renamed Ohio Knitting Mills in 1947, the company had easily transitioned to the world of women's separates, due in large part to its lead designer, Elizabeth Foderaro. An Italian-American working girl from Cleveland's West Side, Foderaro had apprenticed under Stone's designers while still in high school. When she was promoted to OKM's lead designer, she already had a keen sense of American women's needs and wants.

Many of her early designs were simply feminized versions of Stone's standard menswear. Foderaro made sure that Le Petit Pull purred girly daintiness by modifying the Poor Boy, giving it a wider, more delicate neckline, while dramatically cinching in the waist and adding rounded, curvy sleeves in order to accent the female form. The addition of the sleek pencil skirt transforms this project into an entire ensemble, the elements of which can be worn separately or together.

Designed in a wide range of colorful patterns, Le Petit Pull et Amie proved to be a stylishly versatile outfit, appropriate for work or play, and was one of the company's best sellers, heralding an era in which knitwear would become a dominant form of dress.

A **challenging two-part** design. The top will have you working cables and neck and dolman shaping all at once. Knit on its own, the skirt is less challenging than the full set, and is a versatile piece to wear.

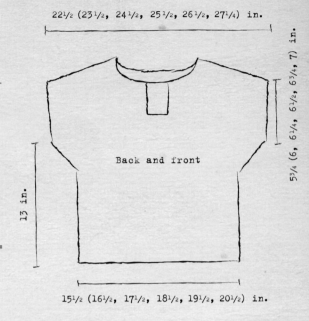

22½ (23½, 24½, 25½, 26½, 27¼) in.

5¾ (6, 6¼, 6½, 6¾, 7) in.

13 in.

Back and front

15½ (16½, 17½, 18½, 19½, 20½) in.

NEEDLES
U.S. size 7 (4.5 mm) straight needles
U.S. size 5 (3.75 mm) straight needles
Adjust needle sizes as needed to obtain gauge.

NOTIONS
Stitch holder
Cable needle
Tapestry needle
Two size 2 sew-on snaps
Three ½-inch mother-of-pearl buttons
Needle and thread
7-inch closed-end zipper

GAUGE
20 sts and 28 rows = 4 inches/10 cm in St st on larger needles

Le Petit Pull Top
SIZES
To fit bust 30 (32, 34, 36, 38, 40) inches

FINISHED MEASUREMENTS
Bust 31¼ (32¾, 35¼, 36¾, 39¼, 40¾) inches
Length 22½ (22¾, 23, 23½, 24, 24½) inches

YARN
Classic Elite Classic One Fifty (100% wool; 150 yds per 50 g)
MC: #7220 Blue Sky, 6 (6, 7, 7, 8, 8) skeins
CC1: #7288 Mango, 1 skein
CC2: #7202 Daisy, 1 skein
CC3: #7201 White, 1 skein

STITCH INSTRUCTIONS
Cable A
Worked over 6 sts
Row 1 (RS): p1, sl 2 to cable needle (cn) and hold to back of work, k2, k2 from cn, p1.
Rows 2, 4, 6, 8, 10 (WS): k1, p4, k1.
Rows 3, 5, 7, 9 (RS): p1, k4, p1.
Rep Rows 1–10.

Cable B
Worked over 8 sts
Row 1 (RS): p1, sl 3 to cn and hold to back of work, k3, k3 from cn, p1.
Rows 2, 4, 6, 8, 10, 12, 14, 16, 18, 20 (WS): k1, p6, k1.
Rows 3, 5, 7, 9, 11, 13, 15, 17, 19 (RS): p1, k6, p1.
Rep Rows 1–20.

Et Amie Skirt
SIZES
To fit hip 32 (34, 36, 38, 40, 42) inches

FINISHED MEASUREMENTS
Hip 33½ (35½, 37½, 39½, 41½, 43½) inches
Length 25 inches

YARN
Classic Elite Classic One Fifty (100% wool; 150 yds per 50 g)
#7220 Blue Sky, 6 (7, 7, 8, 8, 9) skeins

STITCH INSTRUCTIONS
Cable A
Worked over 6 sts

Row 1 (RS): p1, sl 2 to cable needle (cn) and hold to back of work, k2, k2 from cn, p1.
Rows 2, 4, 6, 8, 10 (WS): k1, p4, k1.
Rows 3, 5, 7, 9 (RS): p1, k4, p1.
Rep Rows 1–10.

Cable B
Worked over 8 sts
Row 1 (RS): p1, sl 3 to cn and hold to back of work, k3, k3 from cn, p1.
Rows 2, 4, 6, 8, 10, 12, 14, 16, 18, 20 (WS): k1, p6, k1.
Rows 3, 5, 7, 9, 11, 13, 15, 17, 19 (RS): p1, k6, p1.
Rep Rows 1–20.

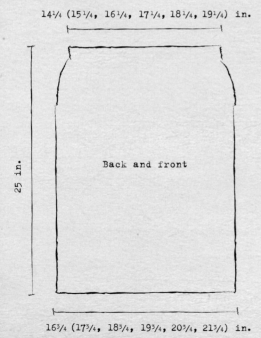

14¼ (15¼, 16¼, 17¼, 18¼, 19¼) in.

25 in.

Back and front

16¾ (17¾, 18¾, 19¾, 20¾, 21¾) in.

Le Petit Pull Top Pattern

BACK
With MC and smaller needles, cast on 80 (84, 90, 94, 100, 104) sts. Work k1, p1 rib for 28 rows. Change to larger needles and continue in St st until piece measures 9½ inches from cast-on edge, ending with a WS row.

Shape Sleeves
Inc 1 st at each end of next row and every following RS row to 110 (114, 120, 124, 130, 134) sts. Place a marker in end of last row to mark base of sleeve.
    Work 6 rows even.
    Inc 1 st at each end of next row and following the 20th row—114 (118, 124, 128, 134, 138) sts total.
    Work even until outside edge of sleeve measures 5¾ (6, 6¼, 6½, 6¾, 7) inches, ending with a WS row.

Shape Neck and Shoulders
Bind off 3 sts at beg of next 8 rows—90 (94, 100, 104, 110, 114) sts rem.
Next row (RS): Bind off 3 sts, k until there are 35 (37, 39, 40, 43, 44) sts on right-hand needle; turn work, placing rem sts on holder.

Right Shoulder
Row 1 (WS): Bind off 3 sts, p to end.
Row 2 (RS): Bind off 3 sts, k to end.
Row 3: Rep Row 1.
Row 4: Bind off 3 sts, k to last 2 sts, k2tog.

Row 5: p2tog, p to end.
    Rep Rows 4 and 5, then Row 4 once more—12 (14, 16, 17, 20, 21) sts rem.
Next row: Purl.
Next row: Bind off 3 sts, k to end.
    Rep the last 2 rows 3 (3, 3, 4, 5, 6) times more.
    Bind off rem 0 (2, 4, 2, 2, 0) sts.
    Join yarn to rem 52 (54, 58, 61, 64, 67) sts with RS facing. Bind off 14 (14, 16, 18, 18, 20) sts for back neck, k to end—38 (40, 42, 43, 46, 47) sts rem.

Left Shoulder
Row 1 (WS): Bind off 3 sts, p to end.
Row 2 (RS): Bind off 3 sts, k to end.
Rows 3 and 4: Rep Rows 1 and 2.
Row 5: Bind off 3 sts, p to last 2 sts, p2tog tbl.
Row 6: ssk, k to end.
    Rep Rows 5 and 6, then Row 5 once more—12 (14, 16, 17, 20, 21) sts rem.
Next row: Knit.
Next row: Bind off 3 sts, p to end.
    Rep the last 2 rows 3 (3, 3, 4, 5, 6) times more.
    Bind off rem 0 (2, 4, 2, 2, 0) sts.

FRONT
With MC and smaller needles, cast on 80 (84, 90, 94, 100, 104) sts. Work k1, p1 rib for 28 rows. Change to larger needles and continue in St st until piece measures 5 inches from cast-on edge, ending with a WS row.

Cable setup row 1 (RS): k54 (56, 60, 62, 66, 68), work Cable B patt over next 8 sts, k18 (20, 22, 24, 26, 28).

Cable setup row 2 (WS): p18 (20, 22, 24, 26, 28), work Cable B patt over next 8 sts, p to end.

Continue as set by last 2 rows until you have completed Row 20 of Cable B patt.

Cable setup row 3 (RS): k46 (48, 52, 54, 58, 60), work Cable A patt over next 6 sts, k2, work Cable B patt over next 8 sts, k18 (20, 22, 24, 26, 28).

Cable setup row 4 (WS): p18 (20, 22, 24, 26, 28), work Cable B patt over next 8 sts, p2, work Cable A patt over next 6 sts, p to end.

Continue as set by last 2 rows until you have completed 4 repeats (40 rows) of Cable A patt.

Cable setup row 5 (RS): k46 (48, 52, 54, 58, 60), work Cable A patt over next 6 sts, k2, work Cable B patt over next 8 sts, k2, work Cable A patt over next 6 sts—k10 (12, 14, 16, 18, 20) sts rem.

Cable setup row 6 (WS): p10 (12, 14, 16, 18, 20), work Cable A patt over next 6 sts, p2, work Cable B patt over next 8 sts, p2, work Cable A patt over next 6 sts, p to end.

AT THE SAME TIME, when piece measures 9½ inches from cast-on edge, shape sleeves as for Back.

AT THE SAME TIME, when outside edge of sleeve measures 2¾ (3, 3, 3¼, 3¼, 3½) inches (112 [116, 122, 126, 132, 136] sts), shape neck:

Row 1 (RS): k49 (51, 54, 56, 59, 61), use backward loop method to cast on 14 sts. Turn, placing rem sts on holder—63 (65, 68, 70, 73, 75) sts total.

Row 2 (WS): (p1, k1) seven times, p to end.

Row 3: k to last 14 sts, (p1, k1) seven times.

Continue with rib at neck edge as set by last 2 rows, remembering to continue sleeve shaping as for Back. When outside edge of sleeve measures 5¾ (6, 6¼, 6½, 6¾, 7) inches ending with a WS row, shape neck and shoulders as follows:

Row 1 (RS): Bind off 3 sts, k to last 14 sts, (p1, k1) seven times.

Row 2 (WS): Bind off in rib 14 sts, p to end—47 (49, 52, 54, 57, 59) sts rem.

Row 3: Bind off 3 sts, k to last 2 sts, k2tog—43 (45, 48, 50, 53, 55) sts rem.

Dec 1 st at neck edge of next 10 (10, 11, 8, 6, 7) rows, while continuing to bind off 3 sts at beg of every RS row until 0 (2, 4, 2, 2, 0) sts rem.

Bind off rem sts.

Join yarn to rem 63 (65, 68, 70, 73, 75) sts with RS facing.

Row 1 (RS): (k1, p1) seven times, k to end.

Row 2 (WS): p to last 14 sts, (k1, p1) seven times.

Continue with rib at neck edge as set by last 2 rows, maintaining established cable patts and remembering to continue sleeve shaping as for Back. When outside edge of sleeve measures 5¾ (6, 6¼, 6½, 6¾, 7) inches ending with a RS row, shape neck and shoulders as follows:

Row 1 (WS): Bind off 3 sts, p to last 14 sts, (k1, p1) seven times.

Row 2 (RS): Bind off in rib 14 sts, k to end—47 (49, 52, 55, 57, 59) sts rem.

Row 3: Bind off 3 sts, p to last 2 sts, p2tog tbl—43 (45, 48, 51, 53, 55) sts rem.

Dec 1 st at neck edge of next 10 (10, 11, 8, 6, 7) rows, while continuing to bind off 3 sts at beg of every WS row until 0 (2, 4, 2, 2, 0) sts rem.

Bind off rem sts.

FINISHING

Block pieces.

Sew shoulder/top of sleeve seams.

Sleeve Ribbing

With MC and smaller needles, RS facing, pick up and knit 2 sts for every 3 rows along outside edge of sleeve, ending with an even number of sts. Work k1, p1 rib for 8 rows. Change to CC3, rib 2 rows. Change to CC2, rib 2 rows. Change to CC1, rib 4 rows. Bind off in rib.

Repeat for second sleeve.

Collar

With MC and smaller needles, WS facing, pick up and knit 1 st in every bound-off st and 2 sts for every 3 rows around neck. Do not include the 14 placket sts at each end. Work in k1, p1 rib for 20 rows. Change to CC3 and work k1, p1 rib for 2 rows. Change to CC2 and work k1, p1 rib for 2 rows. Change to CC1 and work k1, p1 rib for 4 rows. Bind off in rib.

Sew side, sleeve, and sleeve ribbing seams. Tuck the right placket under the left and, with yarn threaded on a tapestry needle, slip-stitch in place. Sew snaps onto placket, then buttons on RS of right placket over snaps. Weave in ends.

Et Amie Skirt Pattern

BACK

With larger needles, cast on 86 (96, 106, 116, 126, 136) sts. Work 6 rows of k1, p1 rib. Continue in St st until piece measures 21 inches from cast-on edge, ending with a WS row.

Shape Hip

Dec row (RS): k1, ssk, k to last 3 sts, k2tog, k1—84 (94, 104, 114, 124, 134) sts rem.

Rep Dec row on every 6th row until 74 (84, 94, 104, 114, 124) sts rem.

Waistband

Change to smaller needles and work even for 20 rows.

Bind off loosely.

FRONT

With larger needles, cast on 86 (96, 106, 116, 126, 136) sts. Work 6 rows of k1, p1 rib. Purl 1 row (WS).

Cable setup row 1 (RS): k52 (60, 68, 76, 84, 92), work Cable A patt over next 6 sts, k2, work Cable B patt over next 8 sts, k2, work Cable A patt over next 6 sts, k10 (12, 14, 16, 18, 20).

Cable setup row 2 (WS): p10 (12, 14, 16, 18, 20), work Cable A patt over next 6 sts, p2, work Cable B patt over next 8 sts, p2, work Cable A patt over next 6 sts, p52 (60, 68, 76, 84, 92).

Continue as set by last 2 rows until you have completed 9 repeats of the leftmost Cable A patt. Work Row 1 of Cable A patt once more, then work these 6 sts in St st while continuing to work the other Cable A and Cable B patts until you have completed 14 repeats of first Cable A. Work Row 1 of Cable A patt once more, then work these 6 sts in St st while continuing to work Cable B patt until you have completed 8 repeats of Cable B. Work Row 1 of Cable B patt once more, then continue working all sts in St st.

AT THE SAME TIME, when piece measures 21 inches from cast-on edge, work hip shaping and waistband as for Back. When waistband is complete, bind off loosely.

FINISHING

Block pieces.

Sew right side seam. Fold top 10 rows at waist to WS and, with yarn threaded on a tapestry needle, slip-stitch in place to create waistband. Insert zipper into top of left side seam. Sew remainder of left side seam. Weave in ends.

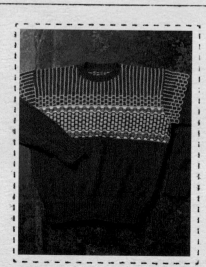

Winter Wonderland

Marc Frisch felt like a kid in a candy store. It was 1945 when the twenty-two-year-old came back from the war, ready to go back to college, and he was being treated by his uncle, Harry Stone, to his choice of any sweater in the Stone Knitting Mills warehouse. "I'd go down there and I could pick out whatever I wanted," Frisch, now eighty-seven years old, remembers fondly.

As he perused the plethora of men's sportswear, from knit T-shirts to graphically patterned pullovers, it was an elaborately detailed ski sweater that caught Frisch's eye. "They made these beautiful ski sweaters—really nice jacquard ones," he says. "I had a girlfriend at school and I got her and myself matching sweaters. I would wear gray slacks and she would wear a gray skirt and we'd walk around, holding hands in our sweaters. We looked really sharp."

Frisch wasn't the only one to covet Stone Knitting Mills' ski sweaters. They were always popular with customers, from Montgomery Ward to Spiegel. In fact, the company's two best-selling designs were dubbed the "Lonesome Pine" and the "Golden Goose." Both were thickly woven woolens with outdoorsy-themed graphics splayed across the chest—picture the iconic reindeer hopping between pine trees or geese in flight over an abstract marsh. Stone sold many of these through the famed sportswear outfitter McGregor.

The Winter Wonderland captures America's new freedom from constraint. Just like the New American Gentleman, this sweater's vibrant mix of colors would have been a novel departure from the muddy bevy of dark hues that described the war era. Worn over a shirt and tie and high-waisted slacks, the Winter Wonderland would lend any outfit an air of casual modernity and playful personality.

As men have further dressed down their closets—replacing the shirt-and-tie ensemble with T-shirts, and high-waisted slacks with jeans—this type of pullover remains a stand-by in every American closet.

This is a classic ski sweater mostly worked in the round, with stranded colorwork. It uses steeks for the neck and armholes.

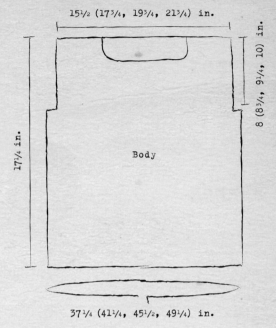

15½ (17¾, 19¾, 21¾) in.

8 (8¾, 9¼, 10) in.

17¼ in.

Body

37¼ (41¼, 45½, 49¼) in.

SIZES
Men's S (M, L, XL)

FINISHED MEASUREMENTS
Chest 37¼ (41¼, 45½, 49¼) inches
Length 25¼ (26, 26½, 27¼) inches

YARN
Classic Elite Classic One Fifty (100% wool; 150 yds per 50 g)
MC: #7255 Scarlet, 8 (9, 10, 11) skeins
A: #7212 Lemon, 1 (1, 1, 2) skeins
B: #7202 Pewter, 2 (2, 2, 3) skeins
C: #7213 Black, 2 (2, 2, 3) skeins

NEEDLES
U.S. size 6 (4 mm) circular needles, 16 inches and 24 or 32 inches long
U.S. size 4 (3.5 mm) circular needle, 24 or 32 inches long
U.S. size 4 double-pointed needles
Adjust needle sizes as needed to obtain gauge.

NOTIONS
Stitch markers
Tapestry needle

GAUGE
24 sts and 32 rows = 4 inches/10 cm in St st on larger needle

NOTES
This sweater is knit in the round, with square inset sleeves, and uses steeks for the armholes and neck. Work the steek sts in vertical stripes (1 st first color, 1 st second color, repeat). The very top of the sleeve is knitted back and forth in rows.

CHART NOTES
Border shows patt rep.
After completing the 66 rnds of Body chart, rep Rnd 66 to end of Body.
After completing the 17 rnds of Sleeve chart, rep Rnd 17 to end of Sleeve.

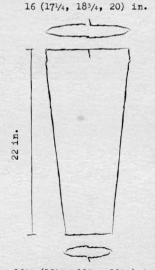

16 (17¼, 18¾, 20) in.

22 in.

10½ (10½, 11½, 11½) in.

BODY

With smaller circular needle and MC, cast on 224 (248, 272, 296) sts. Place marker (pm) and join for working in the round. Work k2, p2 rib for 3 inches. Change to longer, larger needle and work in St st until body measures 13¼ (13¼, 13¾, 13¾) inches from cast-on edge.

Next rnd: k112 (124, 136, 148), pm, k to end.

Pattern setup rnd: Work Row 1 of Body chart (see page 30) to marker, sl marker. Work the chart to end of rnd; sl marker. Continue as set until body measures 17¼ inches.

Armhole steek setup 1: Work in patt to 8 sts before marker, bind off 8 sts, remove marker, bind off 8 sts; work in patt to 8 sts before end of rnd, bind off 8 sts, remove marker, bind off 8 sts.

Armhole steek setup 2: Work in patt to first set of bound-off sts, cast on 5 sts, work in patt to second set of bound-off sts, cast on 5 sts. Place new marker for beg of rnd.

Armhole steek setup 3: Work in patt to first 5 steek sts, work steek sts in vertical stripe pattern (see Notes), work in patt to second 5 steek sts, work steek sts in vertical stripe pattern.

Continue as set by last row until body measures 22 (22½, 23, 24) inches.

Neck steek setup 1: Work 34 (38, 41, 45) sts in patt, bind off center front 28 (32, 38, 42) sts, work 34 (38, 41, 45) sts in patt. Work armhole steek sts, work 96 (108, 120, 132) back sts in patt, work armhole steek sts.

Neck steek setup 2: Work 34 (38, 41, 45) sts in patt, cast on 5 sts, work 34 (38, 41, 45) sts in patt; work to end of round as established.

Next rnd: Work in patt to 3 sts before neck steek sts, k2tog, k1, work 5 steek sts in vertical stripe patt, k1, ssk, work to end of round in patt—32 (36, 39, 43) sts rem for each front shoulder.

Next rnd: Work even.

Rep the last two rnds 4 times more—28 (33, 36, 40) sts rem for each front shoulder.

Work even until body measures 25¼ (26, 26½, 27¼) inches.

Bind off all sts with MC.

SLEEVES

With dpn and MC, cast on 64 (64, 68, 68) sts; pm and join for working in the round. Work k2, p2 rib for 3 inches. Change to shorter, larger circular needle and continue in St st. Work 4 rnds even.

Inc rnd: k1, m1, work to last st, m1, k1—66 (66, 70, 70) sts.

Rep Inc rnd on every following 5th (5th, 5th, 4th) rnd to 96 (104, 112, 120) sts.

Work even until sleeve measures 18½ inches.

Begin working Sleeve chart (see page 30).

When sleeve measures 20¾ inches, turn work at beg-of-rnd marker and begin working back and forth in rows.

When sleeve measures 22 inches, bind off with MC.

FINISHING

Reinforce steeks and cut (see page 153).

Seam right shoulder.

Beg at left front shoulder with smaller circular needle, MC, and RS facing, pick up and knit 3 sts for every 4 rows and 1 st for every st around neck edge. Adjust as necessary to achieve a multiple of 4 sts + 2. Work in k2, p2 rib for 1 inch. Bind off loosely.

Seam left shoulder and neckband. Set sleeves into armholes. Tack steeks down on WS (see page 153). Weave in ends. Block.

Body

8 7 6 5 4 3 2 1

66 65 64 63 62 61 60 59 58 57 56 55 54 53 52 51 50 49 48 47 46 45 44 43 42 41 40 39 38 37 36 35 34 33 32 31 30 29 28 27 26 25 24 23 22 21 20 19 18 17 16 15 14 13 12 11 10 9 8 7 6 5 4 3 2 1

8 7 6 5 4 3 2 1

17 16 15 14 13 12 11 10 9 8 7 6 5 4 3 2 1

Sleeve

MARVELOUS MACHINES

From the abstract snowflakes of the Winter Wonderland to the ethnic honeycomb of Earth Mother, the signature knits of the Ohio Knitting Mills wouldn't have been possible without the company's warp knitting machines.

While there are three types of warp knitting machines—including Milanese and Tricot, which often are used to make lingerie—it was the Raschel machine that was responsible for the majority of the Mills' most dynamic sweaters. This type of warp knitting first creates a lace-like base of thin yarn through which heavier yarns are then knit. This gives the sweater a substantial quality without being too heavy. An ideal approach for creating outerwear, this multilayered fabric also allowed for the richly textured surfaces and infinitely varied graphic patterns that made Ohio Knitting Mills garments so distinctive.

The Raschel machines were composed of flat knitting beds, up to ten feet in width, with anywhere from seven to twenty-four needles every two inches. Each of the needles holds an individual yarn end. Dozens of these machines lined the factory floor. From the ceiling were mounted sorting racks that held numerous cones of yarn whose strands were threaded through the machines, creating an incredible rainbow of colors and textures that hung overhead. With so much yarn required for the Raschel technique, there could be more than one million pounds of yarn stored at the mill at any one time during periods of peak production. And it took incredible manpower to keep these machines running efficiently. While women in calico dresses and work aprons replaced broken needles and restocked thread, male mechanics tended to balancing and repairing the machines, which ran up to sixteen hours a day.

Of particular importance were the men responsible for enabling

Circular Philadelphia Jacquard knitting machines from 1957.

Though Ohio Knitting Mills was one of the country's largest warp knitting operations, the mill didn't rely solely on its Raschel machines. During the early 1940s, the company purchased Philadelphia Jacquard machines, which were largely used to create durable fabrics for its military contracts during the war years. Later, these machines continued to spin out iconic consumer textiles, like Mondrian Skyline. In addition to the rows of Raschel and Jacquard machines, OKM also ran an entirely separate department of more than sixty circular machines, which pumped out large tubes of fabric, hence the name "circular." These machines were responsible for creating finer knits for items like the company's best-selling Poor Boy, as well as a wide variety of trimming and cuffs used to finish the garments sewn from the elaborate fabrics made by the Mills.

These complex mechanical wonders were the engines at the heart of Ohio Knitting Mills, and in many ways extensions of the hands of the craftsmen like Tom and Jules, who created the company's many products. It was as hard for the Rand family to say good-bye to its machines as it was to its workers. When the company sold off its equipment to various buyers in 2003, Gary Rand said he couldn't bear to be in the building as the machines were scrapped. "The sound of them clanking on the metal and the bending of the steel made my stomach turn," Gary recalls.

Today, the Raschel technique is virtually extinct, having been replaced by high-speed circular, full-fashion, and flat knitting machines, as well as by other cheaper forms of production. And sadly, the boldly graphic and richly textured fabrics they created have become quite rare in today's world of apparel.

these machines to work their magic. Tom Rovas (pictured on page x) and, later, Jules O'Hyde were OKM's Raschel knitting engineers. It was their craftsmanship and understanding of how the complex Raschel machines worked that allowed designer Elizabeth Foderaro's ideas to jump off the pages of her sketchpad and become reality.

One could argue, in fact, that it was the technical virtuosity of these men, who coaxed these elaborate designs from their machines, that kept the Ohio Knitting Mills so profitable for so long. As other garment manufacturers struggled to keep up with the rapidly changing styles of the times, OKM was able to adapt to finicky trends, especially in the 1960s and '70s, when consumers demanded knits in boisterous color schemes and quirky fabrics.

OHIO KNITTING MILLS
Original Design

Spring 19 48

4201 PERKINS AVENUE
CLEVELAND, O. 44103

The Poor Boy

Nothing says "American sportswear" more than the Ohio Knitting Mills Poor Boy. With its comfortably cool and colorful fabric and contemporary short-sleeve cut, The Poor Boy quickly became a staple of the era's new, relaxed lifestyle.

The Poor Boy had been in production since the company began under the Stone name in 1927. In fact, it was one of only three styles—including the pullover and the cardigan—that Stone Mills produced in its first two decades of existence. A cotton version of the standard pullover, The Poor Boy was not only cheaper to produce, thanks to its lightweight knit and shortened sleeves, but it also kept the Mills open for production beyond the fall and winter seasons. It was also the perfect canvas for the technical knitting artistry of the Stone Knitting Mills, whose circular warp machines were capable of an infinite array of designs and bold color combinations.

By the time Stone Knitting Mills had been renamed Ohio Knitting Mills in 1947, sportswear was gaining equal acceptance with suits and dresses as postwar America's preferred mode of attire, and The Poor Boy was more popular than ever. The design soon became the uniform of cool, seen on tough guys, from jazz musicians to athletes.

But these knit Ts weren't only popular among American men—they were all the rage in Europe, too. As the United States was pulling itself out of the war era, Europe was rebuilding its cities, searching for a mixture of old and new identities amid the rubble. As America aided in the reconstruction effort, American casualness was embraced throughout Europe, making sportswear pieces like The Poor Boy a fashion staple.

It was through the revival of French and Italian cinema and fashion that The Poor Boy was then reflected back to American audiences in such films as *The Bicycle Thief*, where it was styled with a neck scarf and matching beret, giving the knit shirt the panache of European romance. Before long, The Poor Boy was as internationally iconic as Gene Kelly dancing on the tables of a French café in *An American in Paris*.

Whether dressed up with a contrasting collar or simply fashioned with its standard ribbed neckline and a sporty array of stripes, The Poor Boy helped build a foundation for American style, including today's T-shirt.

This is a classic men's style from the era redesigned for today's woman. Its use of Stockinette stitch and simple shaping makes it a great beginning project.

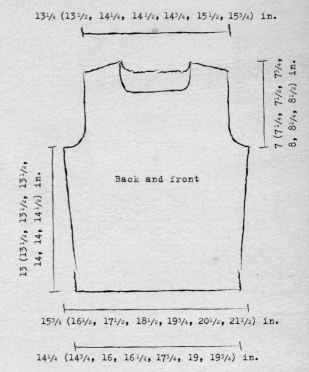

13¼ (13½, 14¼, 14½, 14¾, 15½, 15¾) in.

7 (7¼, 7½, 7¾, 8, 8¼, 8½) in.

Back and front

13 (13½, 13½, 14, 14, 14½) in.

15¾ (16½, 17½, 18½, 19¾, 20½, 21½) in.

14¼ (14¾, 16, 16½, 17¾, 19, 19¾) in.

SIZES
To fit bust 30 (32, 34, 36, 38, 40, 42) inches

FINISHED MEASUREMENTS
Bust 31½ (33¼, 35, 37, 39½, 41¼, 43) inches
Length 20¾ (21½, 21¾, 22, 22¾, 23, 23¾) inches

YARN
Classic Elite Fresco (60% wool, 30% baby alpaca, 10% angora; 164 yds per 50 g)
MC: #5354 Sweet Lilac, 5 (5, 5, 6, 6, 6, 7) skeins
CC1: #5301 Parchment, 1 (1, 1, 2, 2, 2, 2) skeins
CC2: #5371 Purple Haze, 1 skein

NEEDLES
U.S. size 5 (3.75 mm) straight needles
U.S. size 3 (3.25 mm) straight needles
Adjust needle sizes as needed to obtain gauge.

NOTIONS
Stitch holder
Tapestry needle

GAUGE
26 sts and 35 rows = 4 inches/10 cm in St st on larger needles, blocked

NOTES
With both alpaca and angora content, this yarn will bloom and relax with wet-blocking. Be sure to block your swatch!

STITCH INSTRUCTIONS
Stripe Sequence for Body
1½ inches CC1
½ inch MC
1½ inches CC2
CC1 to end of piece

Stripe Sequence for Sleeves
¾ inch CC1
¼ inch MC
¾ inch CC2
MC to end of piece

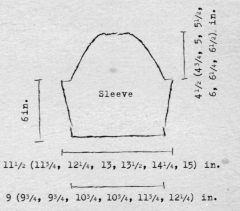

4½ (4¾, 5, 5½, 6, 6½) in.

6 in.

Sleeve

11½ (11¾, 12¼, 13, 13½, 14¼, 15) in.

9 (9¾, 9¾, 10¾, 10¾, 11¾, 12¼) in.

BACK

With smaller needles and MC, cast on 94 (98, 106, 110, 118, 126, 130) sts. Work in k2, p2 rib (beg and end with k2) for 2½ inches. Change to larger needles and work in St st, beg with a WS (purl) row. Work 7 rows even.

Inc row (RS): k2, m1, knit to last 2 sts, m1, k2—96 (100, 108, 112, 120, 128, 132) sts.

Rep Inc row on every following 14th row to 104 (110, 116, 122, 130, 136, 142) sts.

Work even until back measures 13 (13½, 13½, 13½, 14, 14, 14½) inches from cast-on edge, ending with a WS row.

Shape Armholes

Bind off 6 (6, 7, 7, 7, 8, 8) sts at beg of next 2 rows—92 (98, 102, 108, 116, 120, 126) sts rem.

Dec 1 st at each end of next row and on every following RS row until 88 (90, 94, 96, 98, 102, 104) sts rem.

AT THE SAME TIME, when armholes measure 1 inch, begin Stripe Sequence for Body.

Work even until armholes measure 7 (7¼, 7½, 7¾, 8, 8¼, 8½) inches, ending with a WS row.

Shape Shoulders and Neck

Row 1 (RS): Bind off 8 (8, 9, 9, 9, 10, 10) sts, k until there are 18 (19, 19, 20, 21, 21, 22) sts on right-hand needle; turn work, placing rem sts on a holder.

Row 2 (WS): Bind off 3 sts, p to end.

Row 3: Bind off 8 (8, 8, 9, 9, 9, 10) sts, k to end.

Row 4: Purl.

Bind off rem 7 (8, 8, 8, 9, 9, 9) sts.

Join yarn to rem 62 (63, 66, 67, 68, 71, 72) sts with RS facing.

Row 1 (RS): Bind off 36 (36, 38, 38, 38, 40, 40) sts for back neck, k to end.

Row 2 (WS): Bind off 8 (8, 9, 9, 9, 10, 10) sts, p to end—18 (19, 19, 20, 21, 21, 22) sts rem.

Row 3: Bind off 3 sts, k to end.

Row 4: Bind off 8 (8, 8, 9, 9, 9, 10) sts, p to end.

Row 5: Knit.

Bind off rem 7 (8, 8, 8, 9, 9, 9) sts.

FRONT

Work same as Back until armholes measure 4¾ (5, 5¼, 5½, 5¾, 6, 6¼) inches, ending with a WS row.

Shape Neck and Shoulders

Next row (RS): k31 (32, 33, 34, 35, 36, 37) and turn, placing rem sts on a holder.

Next row (WS): Bind off 3 sts, p to end.

Dec row (RS): Knit to 3 sts before neck edge, k2tog, k1—27 (28, 29, 30, 31, 32, 33) sts rem.

Rep Dec row on every following RS row until 23 (24, 25, 26, 27, 28, 29) sts rem.

Work even until armhole measures 7 (7¼, 7½, 7¾, 8, 8¼, 8½) inches, ending with a WS row.

Bind off 8 (8, 9, 9, 9, 10, 10) sts at beg of next row.

Work 1 row even.

Bind off 8 (8, 8, 9, 9, 9, 10) sts at beg of next row.

Work 1 row even.

Bind off rem 7 (8, 8, 8, 9, 9, 9) sts.

Join yarn to rem 57 (58, 61, 62, 63, 66, 67) sts with RS facing.

Next row (RS): Bind off 26 (26, 28, 28, 28, 30, 30) sts for front neck, k to end—31 (32, 33, 34, 35, 36, 37) sts rem.

Next row (WS): Purl.

Next row: Bind off 3 sts, k to end.

Work 1 row even.

Dec row: k1, ssk, k to end—27 (28, 29, 30, 31, 32, 33) sts rem.

Rep Dec row on every following RS row until 23 (24, 25, 26, 27, 28, 29) sts rem.

Work even until armhole measures 7 (7¼, 7½, 7¾, 8, 8¼, 8½) inches, ending with a RS row.

Bind off 8 (8, 9, 9, 9, 10, 10) sts at beg of next row.

Work 1 row even.

Bind off 8 (8, 8, 9, 9, 9, 10) sts at beg of next row.

Work 1 row even.

Bind off rem 7 (8, 8, 8, 9, 9, 9) sts.

SLEEVES

With smaller needles and MC, cast on 62 (66, 66, 70, 70, 78, 82) sts. Work in k2, p2 rib (beg and end with k2) for 1¼ inches.

Change to larger needles. Purl 1 WS row with MC, then begin Stripe Sequence for Sleeves. Work 2 rows even.

Inc row (RS): k2, m1, knit to last 2 sts, m1, k2—64 (68, 68, 72, 72, 80, 84) sts.

Rep Inc row on every following 4th row to 76 (78, 82, 86, 90, 94, 98) sts.

Work even until sleeve measures 6 inches, ending with a WS row.

Shape Cap

Bind off 6 (6, 7, 7, 7, 8, 8) sts at beg of next 2 rows—64 (66, 68, 72, 76, 78, 82) sts rem.

Dec 1 st at each end of next row and on every following RS row until 28 sts rem.

Bind off 2 sts at beg of next two rows.

Bind off 3 sts at beg of next two rows.

Bind off rem 18 sts.

FINISHING

Block pieces.

Seam right shoulder.

With MC and smaller needles, RS facing, beg at left front shoulder, pick up and knit 3 sts for every 4 rows and 1 st in every bound-off st around neckline, ending with a multiple of 4 sts + 2. Work in k2, p2 rib for 1 inch. Bind off in rib loosely.

Seam left shoulder and neckband.

Set sleeves into armholes.

Sew side and sleeve seams.

Weave in ends.

POOR BOY SHIRTS

A sports shirt for Americans of every class

Before World War II, lightweight tennis tops and golf shirts had been associated with the leisure class. As the middle class expanded after the war, OKM began making a tight-fitting cotton shirt for everyone, dubbed the Poor Boy. It typically had short sleeves, a slim silhouette, and a short torso, and it was finished with a banded waist that paired elegantly with the high-waisted trousers popular in the postwar era. OKM offered variants on the classic Poor Boy, with long sleeves, crewnecks, collars, or even keyhole front plackets.

PROJECTS IN THIS CHAPTER

The *The* **1950s**

KNITTING THE AMERICAN DREAM

From Levittown to the suburbs of Southern California, the 1950s were circumscribed by conservatism and conformity. As families filled up newly built rows of tract homes, shows like *The Adventures of Ozzie and Harriet* appeared on television sets weekly, providing a picture-perfect ideal of the American family.

The Eisenhower era was also a time filled with optimism and patriotism. The lives of Middle Americans became inundated with new and exciting gizmos, and people gazed into the future with fervent enthusiasm, dreaming up a utopian world of flying cars, flying saucers (a term coined in 1947), and vacations in space. Even Disneyland, which opened in 1955, offered visitors its own idealized version of the future in Tomorrowland.

Not everyone was enamored with the cookie-cutter values of the nuclear family. The 1950s also gave birth to a number of subcultures, including the beats, predecessors to the impending boom of 1960s counterculture. However, an even more important and much larger demographic was also finding a voice: the teenager. Thanks to the new disposable incomes of middle-class households, teens now had pocket money to spend on everything from 45s to milkshakes. They were increasingly recognized as a distinct consumer group, and thus companies began to aim advertisements directly at them. And although society may have expected teenagers to behave in certain "authorized" ways, they were increasingly associated with rebellion and rock and roll.

Now under the leadership of Leonard Rand, the Ohio Knitting Mills sought to satisfy all tastes. The company was busy fabricating pieces to accommodate everyone from bebop lovers to Boy Scouts. From tidy powder-blue V-necks to vibrant, ultramodern pieces, OKM created expressive and distinct designs to suit each tribe.

OHIO KNITTING MILLS

Original Design

Winter   19 59

4701 PERKINS AVENUE
CLEVELAND, O. 44103

Suburban Sci-Fi

By the the 1950s, America was booming with babies, suburbs, consumerism, and anticommunism. Dwight D. Eisenhower's presidential victory in 1952 marked a sharp return to old-fashioned social values—family-appropriate sit-coms like *I Love Lucy* and *Dennis the Menace* monopolized the small screen, and Disneyland, the manufactured world of cal-culated perfection, was a prime vacation destination.

Although the times signaled a return to conservatism, it was also an era defined by futurist fascination. America's imagination was captivated by space exploration and the infinite possibilities of new technologies and otherworldly discoveries. Almost everything was designed with a space-age sensibility—from rocketlike cars to 3-D cinema. Reports of UFO sightings became increasingly more common as the silver screen exploded with films about life on other planets.

At this cultural intersection of domestic quaintness and sci-fi weirdness was the Suburban Sci-Fi. With its built-in turtleneck and bright yellow trim, it was designed to be "appropriate" for the everyday responsibilities of a home-maker—a wholesome piece that could easily translate from playground to PTA board meeting. It's also an economical piece, forgoing any need for heavy layering or accessories by employing decorative details much like built-in jewelry—a practical quality that not only addresses the variety of a housewife's roles, but also suggests a futurist sensibility of simplicity as well. With its checkered print, luxurious use of mohair, and spaceship-uniform shape, this sweater screams '50s space-age camp—NASA-inspired moon-wear to sport at the grocery store. It's the essence of how people in that decade envisioned the future—proper yet quirky, uncluttered, and oddly functional.

Today, this number is uniquely nostalgic—a relic of a time when people looked ahead with unbridled hope, imagination . . . and unusual color schemes. Slip into this sweater's bubblegum palette and you're ready for a trip to Tomorrowland!

A more challenging project that combines stranded color with intarsia; but with the playful trim and brushed hand of mohair yarn, it's so worth it!

SIZES
To fit bust 32 (36, 41, 45) inches

FINISHED MEASUREMENTS
Bust 34¼ (39, 43, 47½) inches
Length 22¼ (23¼, 24¼, 25¼) inches

YARN
Classic Elite La Gran (76½% mohair, 17½% wool, 6% nylon; 90 yds per 42 g)
A: #6540 Honeydew, 9 (11, 12, 13) balls
B: #6567 Aqua Tint, 9 (11, 12, 13) balls

Cascade Yarns Cascade 220 (100% wool; 220 yds per 100 g)
C: #8010 Natural, 2 skeins

NEEDLES
U.S. size 6 (4 mm) straight needles
U.S. size 6 (4 mm) circular needle, 16 inches long
Adjust needle sizes as needed to obtain gauge.

NOTIONS
Tapestry needle
2–3 yds narrow braid or trim (we used ½-inch #80124 Rayon Scroll Braid, from M&J Trimming)
Needle and thread to match trim

GAUGE
18 sts and 22 rows = 4 inches/10 cm in St st over check pattern

NOTES
This pattern uses both stranded colorwork and intarsia. The sleeves and most of the body are worked in stranded colorwork; the white neck piece is added using intarsia.

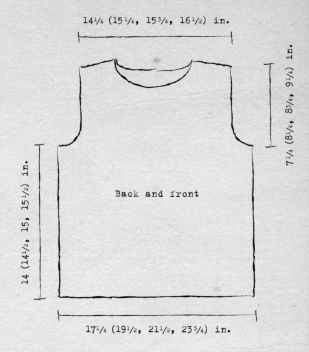

14¼ (15¼, 15¾, 16½) in.

7¼ (8¼, 8¾, 9¼) in.

Back and front

14 (14½, 15, 15½) in.

17¼ (19½, 21½, 23¾) in.

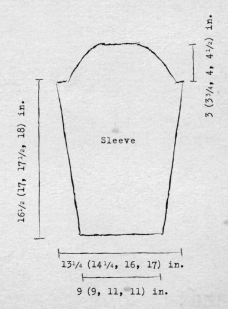

3 (3¾, 4, 4½) in.

Sleeve

16½ (17, 17½, 18) in.

13¼ (14¼, 16, 17) in.

9 (9, 11, 11) in.

BACK

With A and straight needles, cast on 77 (87, 97, 107) sts. Work 3 rows in Garter st.

Next row (RS): Knit, following Row 1 of Main Back chart (right).

Next row (WS): Knit, following Row 2 of Back chart.

Continuing in St st and chart pattern, work 8 rows even. Dec 1 st at each end of next row and every following 10th row two times—71 (81, 91, 101) sts rem. Work 3 rows even. Inc 1 st at each end of next row and every following 8th row 3 times—79 (89, 99, 109) sts total. Work even until piece measures approximately 14 (14½, 15, 15½) inches, ending with Row 6 (9, 12, 3) of chart.

Shape Armholes

Bind off 3 (4, 6, 6) sts at beg of next 2 rows—73 (81, 85, 97) sts rem.

Dec 1 st at each end of next 3 (5, 6, 10) rows—67 (71, 73, 77) sts rem.**

Work even until armhole measures 5 (5½, 6, 6½) inches, ending with Row 9 (3, 9, 3) of chart.

Shape Neck and Shoulders

Follow Back Neck and Shoulder Shaping chart (page 44) for your size.

FRONT

Work same as Back to **, following Main Front chart (right).

Work even until armholes measure 4 (4½, 5, 5½) inches, ending with Row 3 (9, 3, 9) of chart.

Shape Neck and Shoulders

Follow Front Neck and Shoulder Shaping chart (page 45) for your size.

SLEEVES

With A, cast on 42 (42, 52, 52) sts. Work 3 rows in Garter st.

Next row (RS): Knit, following Row 1 of Back chart.

Next row (WS): Knit, following Row 2 of chart.

Continue in St st and chart pattern, work 8 rows even. Inc 1 st at each end of next row and every following 8th (6th, 8th, 6th) row to 62 (66, 74, 78) sts. Work even until piece measures approximately 16½ (17, 17½, 18) inches, ending with Row 6 (9, 12, 3) of chart.

Shape Sleeve Cap

Bind off 3 (4, 6, 6) sts at beg of next 2 rows—56 (58, 62, 66) sts rem.

Work 0 (0, 0, 2) rows even.

Dec 1 st at each end of every row until 18 sts rem.

Bind off.

FINISHING

Weave in ends and block pieces.

Seam shoulders.

Collar

With RS facing, using circular needle and C, beg at shoulder and pick up and knit 3 sts for every 4 rows and 1 st in every bound-off st around neckline, ending with an even number of sts. Work k1, p1 rib in the round for 5 inches. Bind off loosely in rib.

Set sleeves into armholes. Sew side and sleeve seams. Weave in ends and block. Sew trim around neckline, around cuffs, and around front and back above bottom hem. If your trim can be sewn through easily, use an uneven basting stitch (a running stitch with a short stitch showing on the RS of the fabric and a long stitch on the WS) to attach the trim. If the trim is too thick to sew through, couch it in place by oversewing the trim to secure it. Be sure to use thread that matches the color of the trim.

Main Back

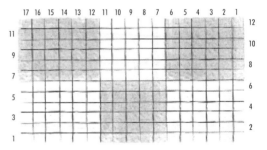

Main Front

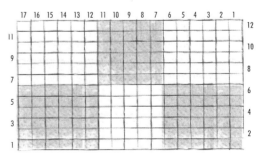

Back Neck and Shoulder Sloping (below) and Front Neck and Shoulder Shaping (opposite).
For charts for size extra-large, go to www.ohioknittingmills.com.

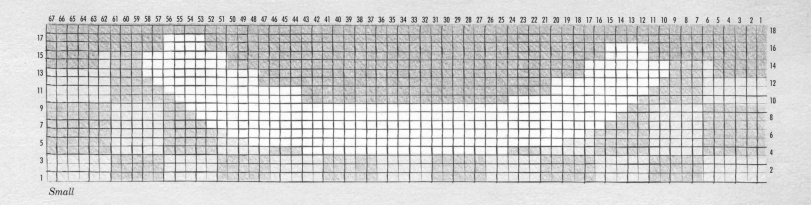

Small

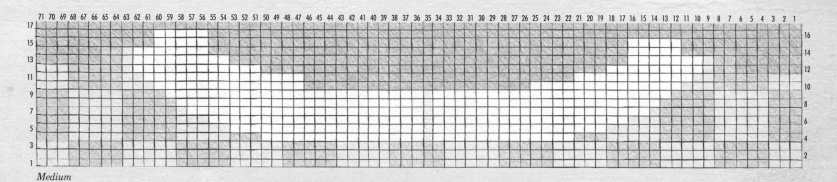

Medium

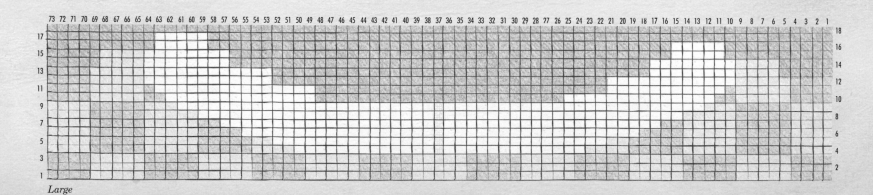

Large

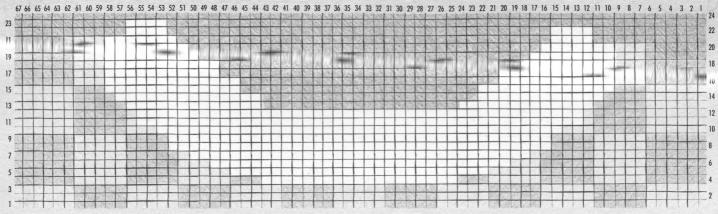

Small

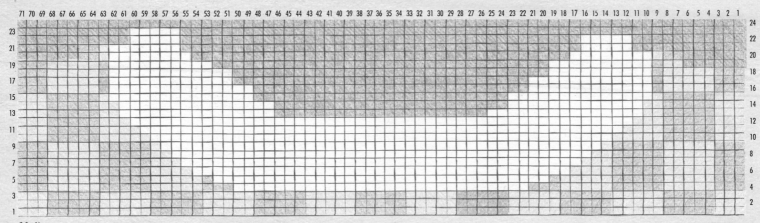

Medium

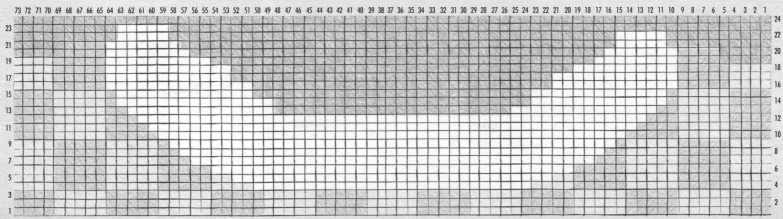

Large

OHIO KNITTING MILLS
Original Design

Fall   19 54

4701 PERKINS AVENUE
CLEVELAND, O. 44103

Father Knows Best

Like the women of the 1950s, men also found that post-
war society was redefining their roles. Many of those who had
gone off to war as blue-collar workers, having gained experience and training in the armed services, returned and found
that additional training enabled them to get better jobs, even
moving into white-collar positions. Their new salaries not
only allowed Mom to stay at home and tend to the kids, but
also afforded Dad more free time on the weekends.

From Boy Scout leaders to Elks Lodge members, fathers
needed a uniform for life outside the office, especially in a
world that emphasized conformity. Nothing says "leisurely
dad" more than Father Knows Best—a V-neck cardigan and
a staple of every great 1950s TV father figure, from *Leave It
to Beaver*'s Ward Cleaver (Hugh Beaumont) to *Father Knows
Best*'s Jim Anderson (Robert Young). Intended to be a quick
swap-out for the suit jacket, the V-neck cardigan maintains
the austerity of a professional man while adding comfort and
mobility. Clad in his cardigan, a man could read the paper,
mow his lawn, or toss the ball around with Junior. Thus the
V-neck cardigan became a wardrobe basic that married the
role of the father with his new life of leisure.

At the same time that the cardigan was becoming a wardrobe staple, the Ohio Knitting Mills began looking toward
more durable and cost-efficient fibers for their sweaters. The
1950s saw the emergence of synthetics, from nylon to poly-
ester, that had been developed during the war and were now
being embraced by corporate America. For example, Orlon, an
acrylic fiber trademarked by Dupont in 1941, was marketed as
wrinkle-free, easy-to-wash, and therefore better than natural
fibers. It reigned supreme in an era where all things new were
automatically considered "improved."

Not only did Father Knows Best come in a large array of
fibers, but its simple structure also allowed for a wide range of
colors and patterns—from an understated baby blue to bright
argyles. Dad could be sure to have a V-neck for every occa-
sion, whether it was golf at the country club or Sunday night
dinner with the family. Versatile and iconic, Father Knows
Best remains one of OKM's best-selling sweaters.

Here's that classic "grandpa sweater" that looked so stylish on Mister Rogers, and now you can wear it too! The pattern is straightforward, so even a modest knitter can complete it.

SIZES
Men's S (M, L, XL)

FINISHED MEASUREMENTS
Chest 34½ (38, 41½, 46) inches
Length 24 (24½, 25¾, 26¼) inches

YARN
Cascade Yarns Cascade 220 (100% wool; 220 yds per 100 g)
#9485 Kentucky Blue, 5 (5, 6, 7) skeins

NEEDLES
U.S. size 7 (4.5 mm) straight needles
U.S. size 5 (3.75 mm) straight needles
Adjust needle sizes as needed to obtain gauge.

NOTIONS
Stitch holders
Spare knitting needle for 3-needle bind-off
Tapestry needle
Six ¾-inch buttons
Needle and thread

GAUGE
20 sts and 28 rows = 4 inches/10 cm in St st on larger needles

STITCH INSTRUCTIONS
Buttonhole
Bind off in rib 4 sts in center of row; on next row, use backward loop or cable method to cast on 4 sts over gap.

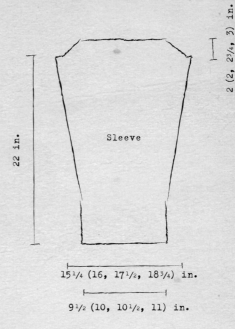

2 (2, 2¾, 3) in.

Sleeve

22 in.

15¼ (16, 17½, 18¾) in.

9½ (10, 10½, 11) in.

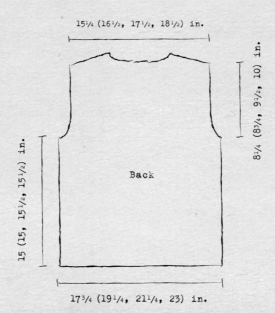

15¼ (16½, 17½, 18½) in.

8¼ (8¾, 9½, 10) in.

15 (15, 15½, 15½) in.

Back

17¾ (19¼, 21¼, 23) in.

4½ (5, 5¼, 5½) in.

Left front

8 (8¾, 9½, 10¾) in.

BACK

With smaller needles, cast on 88 (98, 108, 118) sts. Work k1, p1 rib for 2 inches. Change to larger needles and continue in St st until piece measures 15 (15, 15½, 15½) inches from cast-on edge, ending with a WS row.

Shape Armholes

Bind off 3 (3, 4, 4) sts at beg of next 2 rows—82 (92, 100, 110) sls rem.

Dec 1 st at each end of every 4th (4th, 4th, 2nd) row until 78 (84, 90, 94) sts rem.

Work even until armholes measure 8¼ (8¾, 9½, 10) inches, ending with a WS row.

Shape Shoulders and Neck

Next row (RS): k24 (25, 27, 29), bind off center 30 (34, 36, 36) sts, k to last 9 sts, wrap and turn.

Left Shoulder

Next row (WS): Purl.

Next row (RS): k1, ssk, k to last 17 sts, wrap and turn.

Next row (WS): Purl.

Next row (RS): Knit to end, knitting into and hiding wraps.

Place these 23 (24, 26, 28) sts on holder.

Right Shoulder

Rejoin yarn at neck edge with WS facing.

Next row (WS): Purl to last 9 sts, wrap and turn.

Next row (RS): Knit.

Next row (WS): p1, p2tog, p to last 17 sts, wrap and turn.

Next row (RS): Knit.

Next row (WS): Purl to end, purling into and hiding wraps.

Place these 23 (24, 26, 28) sts on holder.

POCKET LININGS (make 2)

With larger needles, cast on 28 (28, 30, 30) sts. Work in St st for 5½ inches. Break yarn and place sts on holder.

LEFT FRONT

With smaller needles, cast on 42 (46, 50, 56) sts. Work k1, p1 rib for 2 inches. Change to larger needles and continue in St st until piece measures 6¼ (6¼, 6½, 6½) inches from cast-on edge, ending with a WS row.

Pocket

Next row (RS): k7 (9, 10, 13), place next 28 (28, 30, 30) sts on holder, k28 (28, 30, 30) sts of pocket lining, k7 (9, 10, 13).

Continue in St st until piece measures 15 (15, 15½, 15½) inches from cast-on edge, ending with a WS row.

Shape Armhole and Neck

Bind off 3 (3, 4, 4) sts at beg of next row—39 (43, 46, 52) sts rem.

Dec 1 st at armhole edge on every 4th (4th, 4th, 2nd) row 2 (4, 5, 8) times.

AT THE SAME TIME, dec 1 st at neck edge on every 4th row until 23 (24, 26, 28) sts rem.

Work even until armhole measures 8¼ (8¾, 9½, 10) inches, ending with a RS row.

Shape Shoulder

Next row (WS): Purl to last 9 sts, wrap and turn.

Next row (RS): Knit.

Next row: Purl to last 17 sts, wrap and turn.

Next row: Knit.

Next row: Purl to end, purling into and hiding wraps.

Place sts on holder.

RIGHT FRONT

Work as for Left Front, reversing shaping.

SLEEVES

With smaller needles, cast on 50 (52, 54, 56) sts. Work in k1, p1 rib for 5 inches. Change to larger needles and continue in St st; inc 1 st at each end of first row and every following 6th (6th, 4th, 4th) row to 78 (82, 90, 96) sts.

Work even until piece measures 22 inches from cast-on edge, ending with a WS row.

Shape Cap

Bind off 3 (3, 4, 4) sts at beg of next 2 rows—72 (76, 82, 88) sts rem.

Dec 1 st at each end of every row until 48 (48, 44, 44) sts rem.

Bind off.

FINISHING

Block pieces.

Join shoulders using 3-needle bind-off.

Neck/Button Band

With smaller needles, cast on 12 sts. Work in k1, p1 rib for 1½ inches. Make buttonhole.

Continue in rib, making additional buttonholes every 3¼ inches until 6 holes have been made. Continue in rib until strip, when slightly stretched, is long enough to go all around front and neck edges of garment. Bind off. Slip-stitch in place; buttonhole side goes on Left Front. Attach buttons opposite buttonholes.

Pocket Edging

With smaller needles, join yarn to 28 (28, 30, 30) held pocket sts with RS facing. Work in k1, p1 rib for ¾ inch, bind off in rib. Slip-stitch pocket lining in place on WS, taking care not to let sts show through on RS. Sew short ends of pocket edging to sweater.

Set sleeves into armholes. Sew side and sleeve seams. Weave in ends.

A FAMILY AFFAIR

In September 1952 the leaders of the Cleveland knitwear industry gathered to discuss a very grave concern regarding the future of their companies. "The industry is too ingrown," one man complained during the meeting.

The owners of the knitting mills were concerned that not enough new blood was being infused into the industry. "One problem is that the industry is not attracting young men who, in years to come, would be able to take over the management of the mills," argued another trade member. "Most of the firms have their own sons coming up in the business, and there is not much room for others to advance."

Since the beginning of the textile industry in the United States, the so-called needle trades had been a family affair, relying on subsequent generations to carry the torch and take over the businesses. Part of the problem was that these industries had done little to promote themselves and attract recruits into their management sector. While it was easy to find immigrants to work the factory floor, finding people for leadership positions was a different story. Many viewed the "rag trade" as difficult and dirty work, preferring more glamorous jobs than sewing piece goods or operating textile machines. The only option mill owners often had to keep their companies alive was to rely on their sons to take over the business (a precarious dependency, since labor statistics often show that only 15 percent of family-run companies survive the third generation).

The Ohio Knitting Mills was no different. When Harry Stone and Walker Woodworth left the business in the late 1940s, it was their sons and sons-in-law who took hold of the company reins. While Walker's son, Leslie, took control of the Winona Mills, a Minnesota-based knitting operation owned by Stone Knitting, Harry's son-in-law, Leonard Rand, reorganized the Cleveland plant under the Ohio Knitting Mills name.

Meanwhile, Harry's sister had also married into the knitwear trade. Her husband, H. E. Frisch, had worked alongside Harry at the Cleveland-based Rich-Sampliner Knitting Mills Co., where they both got their start in the world of knitwear. After leaving Rich-Sampliner in the mid-1920s, H. E. also started his own company, the Frisch Knitting Mills, which was located just a few floors below the Stone Knitting Mills in the National Screw building on Stanton Avenue.

H. E.'s son Marc remembers working summers during high school for both his father and his uncle in the 1930s. While he would help his father take inventory and weigh the yarn during the day, he'd run the Raschel machines for Stone in the night shift. After serving in World War II and then finishing his college degree, Marc returned to Cleveland and helped to take over the Frisch business. "I didn't like it," Marc recalls. "I did have a choice, but it felt like my fate. And then I got out of it, and that is the greatest thing I ever did."

Marc left his family's business in 1967—just as his cousin Gary Rand was preparing to eventually come into the Ohio Knitting Mills. Gary had been born around the time his father took over the family

Leonad and Gary Rand at Ohio Knitting Mills, early 1990s.

business in 1947. From a young age, it was clear that he would one day be expected to take over for his father. Like Marc, Gary also spent his summers working on his father's factory floor, either sweeping or loading the washing machines with fabric. "I wasn't a happy camper," he recalls, "but it was what I was destined to do."

Gary later graduated from the Philadelphia College of Textile Sciences, and in 1969 he returned to Cleveland to help his father move the Ohio Knitting Mills to its new location in the old Printz-Beiderman building at 1974 East 61st Street. However, it would be a long time before the senior Rand would fully pass the torch to his son. It wasn't until 2001, when Leonard suffered a major stroke, that Gary finally took charge of the company. And by then it was too late to reorganize the business to survive in the NAFTA era of offshore competitors. The following year, the Ohio Knitting Mills received a letter from Pendleton Woolen Mills, their last remaining major customer, informing them that it had found an Asian manufacturer and would no longer need OKM's services. After more than seventy-five years of making knitwear, the Stone-Rand family would no longer operate Ohio Knitting Mills.

OHIO KNITTING MILLS
Original Design

Spring 19_56_

4701 PERKINS AVENUE
CLEVELAND, O. 44103

Saturday Matinee Bolero

As the United States gained superpower status around the world, a patriotic fervor swelled throughout the country. The nation idealized the "American man" as a self-made citizen who, through unwavering morality and hard work, always came out on top. During the war years, this American hero was fighting in the European and Pacific theaters. But once the war ended, a new backdrop for his heroics emerged. Nothing better represented the narrative of the American hero than the story of the American West—a wild, lawless place where the iconic cowboy prevails and restores order and good, old-fashioned values . . . at least in the Hollywood version. From the tumbleweed sounds of Gene Autry to the horseback epics of John Wayne, 1950s America was obsessed with all things Western—the perfect allegory for its newfound superiority.

To cater to the country's cowboy frenzy, the Ohio Knitting Mills was manufacturing pieces like Saturday Matinee Bolero. While most OKM designs focused on function first, this pattern emphasizes the decorative—it's a festive accoutrement for the all-American gal. The vest is intended to round out any outfit with a hint of "Home on the Range" romance. Its Spanish influence, rooted in the American Southwest, where Hispanic culture melded with a cowboy's tangy serenade after the Mexican Cession of 1848, also lends an air of exoticism.

Saturday Matinee Bolero also captures a sense of fantasy and manufactured innocence that was crucial to the 1950s version of the American West. The real American frontier may have been an unforgiving environment, but later it would be neatly packaged into an array of Disneyland attractions, where wholesomeness replaced gruesomeness and the line between the good guys and the bad guys was clearly drawn.

Today, it's easy to mock this rendering of the American West as naïve, but there's something enchanting about the tailored image of the cowboy and his Spanish damsel in distress. Worn over a pair of jeans and a T-shirt, this cropped pattern lends just the right mix of romance and vintage femininity.

The bolero body is quick to knit, with only two short seams to sew up. Applied I-cord finishes the edges. Use our embroidery pattern for its Western-style embellishment or embroider your own design!

SIZES
To fit bust 30 (34, 38, 42, 46) inches

FINISHED MEASUREMENTS
Bust 30 (34, 38, 42, 46) inches
Length 16½ (17, 18, 18½, 19) inches

YARN
Cascade Yarns Cascade 220 (100% wool; 220 yds per 100 g)
MC: #8555 Black, 2 (2, 3, 3, 3) skeins
CC: #8010 Natural, 1 skein

NEEDLES
U.S. size 7 (4.5 mm) circular needle, 24 inches long
Adjust needle size as needed to obtain gauge.

NOTIONS
Large stitch holder or spare circular needle
Tapestry needle
Two U.S. size 6 (4 mm) double-pointed needles
Dressmaker's chalk (optional)

GAUGE
20 sts and 28 rows = 4 inches/10 cm in St st on circular needle

---

NOTES
The bolero is knit flat in one piece to the underarms, then in segments to the shoulders. The circular needle is used to accommodate the large number of stitches.

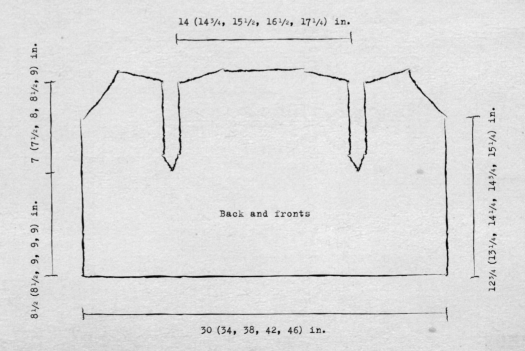

14 (14¾, 15½, 16½, 17¼) in.

7 (7½, 8, 8½, 9) in.

8½ (8½, 9, 9, 9) in.

12¾ (13¼, 14¼, 14¾, 15¼) in.

Back and fronts

30 (34, 38, 42, 46) in.

BODY

With MC and circular needle, cast on 150 (170, 190, 210, 230) sts. Work in St st for 8½ (8½, 9, 9, 9) inches, ending with a WS row.

Upper Right Front

Next row (RS): k38 (43, 48, 53, 58) sts, turn work. Place rem sts on holder or spare needle.

Next row (WS): p1, p2tog, p to end.

Next row (RS): Knit to last 3 sts, k2tog, k1.

Continue to dec 1 st at armhole edge on every row 0 (0, 0, 4, 5) times more, then on RS rows only until 35 (37, 39, 41, 43) sts rem.

Work even until armhole measures 4¼ (4¾, 5¼, 5¾, 6¼) inches, ending with a WS row.

Bind off 3 sts at beg of next row—32 (34, 36, 38, 40) sts rem.

Dec 1 st at neck edge of every row 7 (7, 9, 11, 13) times, then on RS rows only until 19 (21, 22, 23, 24) sts rem.

Bind off 7 (7, 8, 8, 8) sts at beg of next row (WS).

Work 1 row even.

Bind off 6 (7, 7, 8, 8) sts at beg of next row.

Work 1 row even.

Bind off rem sts.

Upper Back

Join yarn to rem sts with RS facing and k74 (84, 94, 104, 114). Turn work, placing rem sts on holder or spare needle.

Next row (WS): p1, p2tog, p to last 3 sts, p2tog tbl, p1.

Next row (RS): k1, ssk, k to last 3 sts, k2tog, k1.

Continue to dec 1 st at each end of every row 0 (0, 0, 4, 5) times more, then on RS rows only until 70 (74, 78, 82, 86) sts rem.

Work even until armhole measures 7 (7½, 8, 8½, 9) inches.

Bind off 7 (7, 8, 8, 8) sts at beg of next 2 rows.

Bind off 6 (7, 7, 8, 8) sts at beg of next 2 rows.

Bind off 6 (7, 7, 7, 8) sts at beg of next 2 rows.

Bind off rem 32 (32, 34, 36, 38) sts.

Upper Left Front

Join yarn to rem 38 (43, 48, 53, 58) sts with RS facing and k to end.

Next row (WS): Purl to last 3 sts, p2tog tbl, p1.

Next row (RS): k1, ssk, k to end.

Continue to dec 1 st at armhole edge on every row 0 (0, 0, 4, 5) times more, then on RS rows only until 35 (37, 39, 41, 43) sts rem.

Work even until armhole measures 4¼ (4¾, 5¼, 5¾, 6¼) inches, ending with RS row.

Bind off 3 sts at beg of next row—32 (34, 36, 38, 40) sts rem.

Dec 1 st at neck edge of every row 7 (7, 9, 11, 13) times, then on RS rows only until 19 (21, 22, 23, 24) sts rem.

Work 1 row even.

Bind off 7 (7, 8, 8, 8) sts at beg of next row (RS).

Work 1 row even.

Bind off 6 (7, 7, 8, 8) sts at beg of next row.

Work 1 row even.

Bind off rem sts.

FINISHING

Seam shoulders.

With CC and dpn, work 4-stitch applied I-cord around all edges.

Weave in ends and block.

Embroidery

Note: All embroidery is done with CC.

Using a single strand, work Outline st to make the swirling and curly lines around the bottom, front, and neckline openings of the bolero (refer to the photograph and the illustrations on page 56). Your stitching should be free-form and fluid. If you find it necessary to have a guide, draw the swirling lines on the fabric with dressmaker's chalk and stitch on top of the marks (see page 56).

Three-Petal Flowers

Again referring to the photo and illustrations, work stems off of the swirling lines for placement of the flowers in Outline st, using a single strand of yarn.

For each flower, work the outer edge of the petals in Outline st. Make the inner petals using a Lazy Daisy st.

Using a double strand of CC, work one French Knot at the center point of each flower, where all the petals meet.

Weave in ends. Block to even out stitching.

Embroidery of three-petal flowers.

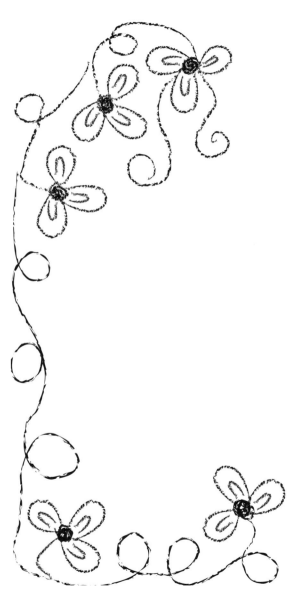

Embroidery Guide for Front

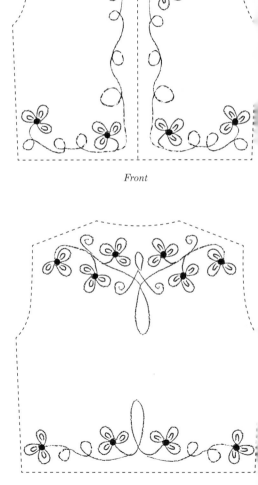

Front

Back

TRACE STITCHING TUTORIAL

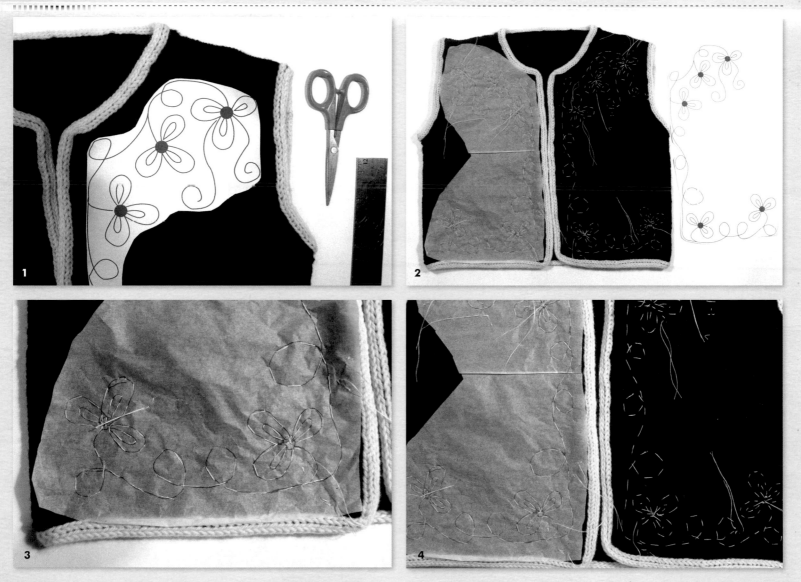

1: Embroidery pattern is photocopied and resized to fit your bolero vest. *2:* The pattern is traced onto tracing paper or thin vellum, which is then positioned on the project so that the pattern lines fall exactly where you would like the embroidery to be. *3:* With a loose running stitch, sew through the tracing and knitting, following the pattern lines—sew through only the front panel. *4:* Carefully remove the tracing paper, leaving just the thread lines, which will be your guide for following the pattern with your embroidery stitching. Once you have completed the embroidery, snip and remove the trace threads, taking care to not cut or disturb your embroidery.

OHIO KNITTING MILLS
Original Design

Winter 19 55

4701 PERKINS AVENUE
CLEVELAND, O. 44103

Mr. Ski Lodge

Central to the identity of 1950s America was the auto-mobile. No longer just a mode of transportation, these chrome-laden dream machines became synonymous with status and the new spending power of the American household. Along with the country's new, overdesigned automobiles came a freshly paved network of extensive interstate highways that could take a family from its home in Cleveland to a ski lodge in the Poconos in less than a day. The road trip became the new American ideal of a family vacation. And Ohio Knitting Mills knew exactly what folks should pack.

Since the early days of Stone Knitting Mills, the ski sweater had always been a big seller. With a rapidly expanding middle class that could now afford a quick weekend trip to the mountains, the company's iconic knitwear was more popular than ever. Like the automobile, the Mr. Ski Lodge sweater was as much a status symbol as it was functional.

Its effortless style and casual graphic design suggest a man of leisure with enough time and cash for a getaway to the slopes.

This sweater perfectly recalls the days when rustic ski lodges and resorts dotted the landscape along the country's new roads and were packed to the rafters with families looking for snow-covered fun. The image of folks swooshing down ski runs and lounging around a roaring fire in their cozy sweaters with cups of hot cocoa became an attainable American dream emblazoned in the pages of magazines and on highway billboards.

Even now, Mr. Ski Lodge strikes the perfect balance between well-groomed stylishness and casual cool—a piece that works just as well at a rock concert as it still does at a mountain resort.

A project that almost any knitter can easily accomplish, made unique and distinctive with a modest number of embroidered embellishments.

SIZES
Men's S (M, L, XL)

FINISHED MEASUREMENTS
Chest 37½ (41½, 44¼, 48) inches
Length 24 (25, 26, 27½) inches

YARN
Patons Classic Wool (100% wool; 223 yds per 100 g)
MC: #00205 Deep Olive, 4 (5, 6, 6) skeins
CC1: #00202 Aran, 2 (2, 3, 3) skeins
CC2: #77117 Worn Denim, 1 skein
CC3: #00238 Paprika, 1 skein

NEEDLES
U.S. size 7 (4.5 mm) straight needles
U.S. size 7 (4.5 mm) circular needle, 16 inches long
Adjust needle sizes as needed to obtain gauge.

NOTIONS
Tapestry needle
Needle and thread
Safety pins

GAUGE
17 sts and 24 rows = 4 inches/10 cm in St st on straight needles

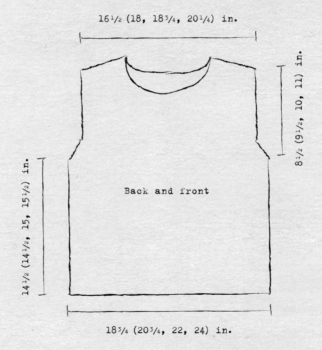

16½ (18, 18¾, 20¼) in.

8¼ (9¼, 10, 11) in.

14½ (14½, 15, 15½) in.

Back and front

18¾ (20¾, 22, 24) in.

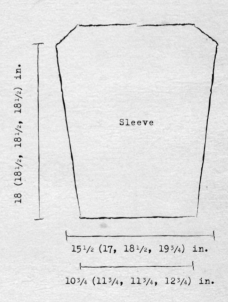

18 (18½, 18½, 18½) in.

Sleeve

15½ (17, 18½, 19¾) in.

10¾ (11¾, 11¾, 12¾) in.

BACK

With straight needles and MC, cast on 82 (90, 98, 106) sts and work k2, p2 rib for 2½ inches, dec 0 (0, 2, 2) sts evenly spaced on last row—82 (90, 96, 104) sts rem. Continue in St st until piece measures 13½ (13½, 14, 14½) inches, ending with a WS row. Change to CC2 and work 6 rows.

Shape Armhole

Dec 1 st at each end of next row and every following RS row until 72 (78, 82, 88) sts rem.

AT THE SAME TIME, when you have worked a total of 10 (10, 12, 12) rows in CC2, change to CC1. Work in CC1 to end of piece.

Work even until armhole measures 7¾ (8¾, 9¼, 10¼) inches, ending with a WS row.

Shape Neck and Shoulders

Next row (RS): k27 (29, 30, 32); turn work, placing rem sts on holder.

Working right shoulder only:

Row 1 (WS): Bind off 4 sts, p to end.
Row 2: Knit.
Row 3: Bind off 2 sts, p to end—21 (23, 24, 26) sts rem.
Row 4: Bind off 4 (5, 5, 5) sts, k to last 2 sts, k2tog.
Row 5: p2tog, p to end.
Rows 6 and 7: Rep Rows 4 and 5—9 (9, 10, 12) sts rem.
Row 8: Bind off 4 (4, 5, 6) sts.
Row 9: Purl.
Bind off rem sts.

Join yarn to rem sts with RS facing. Bind off 18 (20, 22, 24) sts for back neck, k to end.

Complete left shoulder to match right, reversing shaping.

FRONT

Work as for Back until armhole measures 5½ (6½, 7, 7½) inches, ending with a WS row.

Shape Neck

Next row (RS): k30 (32, 33, 35), join second ball of yarn and bind off center 12 (14, 16, 18) sts, k30 (32, 33, 35). Working both sides at the same time with separate balls of yarn, bind off 5 sts at each neck edge once, then dec 1 st at neck edge on every row 5 times, then dec 1 st at each neck edge on every RS row until 17 (19, 20, 22) sts rem. Work even until armholes measure 8½ (9½, 10, 11) inches.

Shape Shoulders

Bind off 4 (5, 5, 5) sts at each armhole edge twice.

Bind off 4 (4, 5, 6) sts at each armhole edge once.

Bind off rem sts.

SLEEVES

With MC, cast on 48 (52, 52, 56) sts and work k2, p2 rib for 2½ inches. Continue in St st, inc 1 st at each end of every 8th (8th, 6th, 4th) row to 68 (74, 80, 86) sts. Work even until sleeve measures 17 (17½, 17½, 17½) inches, ending with a WS row. Change to CC2 and work 6 rows.

Shape Cap

Dec 1 st at each end of every RS row 5 (6, 7, 8) times—58 (62, 66, 70) sts rem.

AT THE SAME TIME, when you have worked a total of 10 (10, 12, 12) rows in CC2, change to CC1. Work in CC1 to end of piece.

Bind off.

FINISHING

Block pieces.
Seam shoulders.
Set in sleeves. Sew side and sleeve seams.

Collar

With circular needle and MC, RS facing, beg at right shoulder, pick up and knit 2 sts for every 3 rows and 1 st in every bound-off st around neck, ending with a multiple of 4 sts. Work k2, p2 rib in the round for 3 inches. Bind off loosely. Fold collar to inside and slip-stitch bound-off edge in place.

Weave in ends.

Embroidery

Note: Each embroidered tree will cover approximately 8 rows. Each 2-Chain-stitch side branch moves at a slight slant over 2 stitches and up 1 row.

Mark

Determine the center-front point of the sweater and mark it with a pin. This will be the stitch that the center embroidered tree will be worked on.

Using a ruler, measure 2¾ (3, 3⅛, 3⅜) inches on either side of the center front and mark. These two points mark two more embroidery points for the second and third trees. Then measure 2¾ (3, 3⅛, 3⅜) inches to the right and left of the second and third points and mark. These mark the fourth and fifth trees.

Bottom Row of Trees

Begin with the embroidery on the CC2 stripe. Referring to the photo (page 58) and the illustration for Tree 1, work in Chain st between the center front stitches to form the center of the tree in CC3 and CC1, as indicated. The embroidery should be centered within the CC2 stripe and be approximately 1¼ inches high. Refer to the illustration for the side branch colors. Complete 5 embroidered trees on the stripe, one at each mark.

Middle Row of Trees

This row of trees should be worked in the yoke of the sweater, directly above the bottom row of trees. Follow the photo (page 58) and the illustration for Tree 2, placing the trees ¼ inch above the color change row.

Top Row of Trees

This row of trees should be worked in the yoke of the sweater, approximately ¾ inch above the middle row of trees. Refer to the photo (page 58) and the illustration for Tree 3 for color placement.

Shoulders

Stitch an embroidered Tree 2 at each shoulder, placing it approximately ¾ inch above the top row of trees. Work one tree in each shoulder.

Sleeves

Determine the center of the sleeve by folding it in half and placing a pin. Stitch one embroidered Tree 2 at the center point. It should begin ¼ inch above the CC1 color change row.

Measure 2 inches on either side of the first sleeve embroidery and mark with a pin. Stitch one embroidered Tree 1 at each of these points in the middle of the CC2 stripe.

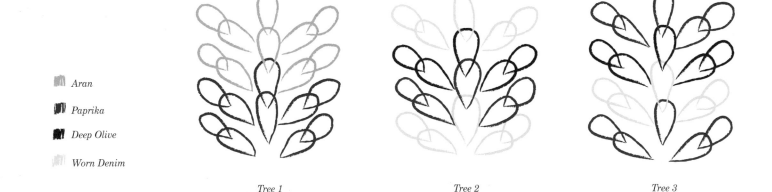

Aran

Paprika

Deep Olive

Worn Denim

Tree 1   Tree 2   Tree 3

SKI SWEATERS

Colorful warmth for the modern outdoor guy

Men's sweaters were the mill's biggest item when it opened in the 1920s. In those days before central heating, sweaters were often worn with a jacket over them—they offered extra warmth as well as a color and texture accent. With the rise of outdoor recreation, and particularly the glamorization of such "European" pursuits like skiing, these sweaters started to be knit of heavier yarns and became more patterned and exuberant.

OHIO KNITTING MILLS
Original Design

Fall 19 56

4701 PERKINS AVENUE
CLEVELAND, O. 44103

The Rebel Rouser

Whether listening to the latest Buddy Holly hit on their AM tuners, cruising Main Street in decked-out hot rods, or eating burgers and fries and drinking strawberry shakes at the local diner, American teenagers in the Eisenhower era knew how to keep busy. From record collectors to fashion fiends, teenagers had become a huge consumer group.

Retailers cashed in on this new demographic by providing their teen customers with a vast array of products, including music, magazines, junk food, and films. Teenagers, with their ample free time and spending money, were as much a marketing phenomenon as a cultural one.

To signal membership in this new social stratum, a new mode of dress also emerged—clothes a little too provocative for children, but also a tad too "fun" for Mom or Dad. A whole new industry developed to satisfy and define the specific fashion needs of teens—from poodle skirts and letterman jackets to jeans and cigarette pants. New labels strictly dedicated to teenage fashion began popping up, while big-name brands like Sears and J. C. Penney also developed unique lines especially for fashionable sixteen-year-olds.

The Ohio Knitting Mills, which had only recently begun designing fashion pieces for women, was now busy developing entirely new lines of teenage-appropriate apparel, which featured garments like The Rebel Rouser. While the color scheme and accent fringe of The Rebel Rouser may have been a little too loud for most adults—and the loose cowl-neck and cropped length just a bit too racy for grade-schoolers—it was the perfect fashion piece in which to spend one's allowance on a drive-in double feature.

The slip stitch pattern produces a double-layer fabric, made even cozier by the 50/50 wool/llama yarn.

SIZES
To fit bust 32 (36, 40, 44) inches

FINISHED MEASUREMENTS
Bust 34½ (38½, 42½, 46½) inches
Length 21½ (22½, 23½, 24¼) inches

YARN
Classic Elite Montera (50% wool, 50% llama; 127 yds per 100 g)
A: #3862 Kingfisher Blue 6 (7, 8, 9) skeins
B: #3816 Lapaz Natural 2 (2, 3, 3) skeins
C: #3832 Puma Magenta 2 (2, 3, 3) skeins
D: #3829 Spring Leaf 1 (1, 1, 2) skeins

NEEDLES
U.S. size 7 (4.5 mm) straight needles
U.S. size 7 (4.5 mm) circular needle, 16 inches long
U.S. size 6 (4 mm) circular needle, 16 inches long
Adjust needle sizes as needed to obtain gauge.

NOTIONS
Stitch holders
Stitch markers
Tapestry needle
Crochet hook for fringing

GAUGE
20 sts and 26 rows = 4 inches/10 cm in Slip stitch patt on larger needles
22 sts and 18 rows = 4 inches/10 cm in k1, p1 rib on larger needles

===

NOTES
Back and front are worked in one continuous piece, beginning at the bottom hem of the back and working over the shoulders down to the bottom hem of the front. The sleeve stitches are then picked up from the body and worked down to the wrist in k1, p1 rib.
Vertical stripes are worked in a Slip stitch pattern using intarsia.

STITCH INSTRUCTIONS
Slip Stitch Pattern
Multiple of 2 sts
Note: Slip all sts purlwise.
Row 1 (RS): *sl1, k1; rep from * to end.
Row 2 (WS): *sl1, p1; rep from * to end.
Rep Rows 1 and 2.

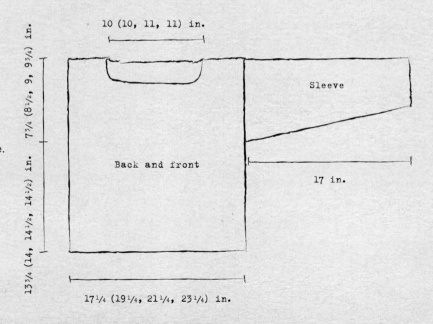

10 (10, 11, 11) in.

7¾ (8½, 9, 9¾) in.

13¾ (14, 14½, 14½) in.

Back and front

Sleeve

17 in.

17¼ (19¼, 21¼, 23¼) in.

BACK AND FRONT

With larger needles and A, cast on 88 (98, 108, 118) sts. Work Garter st for 3 rows.

Setup row for colors (RS): Knit, joining yarns and working sts in colors as follows: 13 (18, 20, 25) sts in A; 8 (8, 10, 10) sts in B; 4 sts in A; 4 sts in C; 4 sts in D; 2 sts in B; 4 sts in A; 10 (10, 12, 12) sts in C; 4 sts in A; 2 sts in B; 4 sts in D; 4 sts in C; 4 sts in A; 8 (8, 10, 10) sts in B; 13 (18, 20, 25) sts in A. Maintain this color arrangement throughout.

Next row (WS): Purl.

Begin working Slip stitch patt. Work even in Slip stitch and vertical stripes until piece measures 21 (22, 23, 23¾) inches from cast-on edge, ending with a WS row.

Shape Back of Neck

Next row (RS): Work 25 (30, 34, 39) sts in patt, place next 38 (38, 40, 40) sts on a holder, work to end of row.

Next row (WS): On first side, work to 6 (6, 8, 8) sts before neck edge, place next 6 (6, 8, 8) sts on neck holder; on second side, place first 6 (6, 8, 8) sts on neck holder, work to end—19 (24, 26, 31) sts rem each side.

Work 1 row even. Place a marker at each end of last row to indicate top of shoulder.

Shape Front of Neck

Work 1 row even.

Being careful to add colors back in the correct sequence, cast on 2 sts at each neck edge 6 times—31 (36, 38, 43) sts. On next RS row, work right shoulder stitches, cast on in colors 26 (26, 32, 32) sts for center front neck, work left shoulder sts—88 (98, 108, 118) sts.

Work even until Front measures same as Back from top of shoulder, finishing bottom edge with 3 rows Garter st as on Back.

Bind off.

COLLAR

With smaller circular needle and A, RS facing, work across 50 (50, 56, 56) held back neck sts in k1, p1 rib, pm, pick up and knit 42 (42, 48, 48) sts evenly around front neck, pm. Work k1, p1 rib for 11 rounds. Change to larger needle.

Next rnd: Work k1, p1 rib, inc 1 st either side of each marker—96 (96, 108, 108) sts.

Next rnd: Work even.

Rep the last 2 rnds until collar measures 6 inches.

Bind off loosely in rib.

SLEEVES

With smaller needles and A, RS facing, pick up and knit 44 (47, 50, 54) sts on either side of shoulder marker, working at a ratio of approximately 3 sts for every 4 rows—88 (94, 100, 108) sts total.

Work in k1, p1 rib, dec 1 st at each end of every 4th row 15 (15, 13, 11) times, then every 2nd row until 48 (52, 56, 60) sts rem. Work even until sleeve measures 17 inches, finishing with 3 rows of Garter st. Bind off.

FINISHING

Sew side and sleeve seams. Weave in ends. Block. Fringe bottom edge with A.

OHIO KNITTING MILLS

Original Design

Winter   19 56

4701 PERKINS AVENUE
CLEVELAND, O. 44103

Abstract Expressionist

As Americans were embracing new modes of design, the art world was likewise exploring radically different types of expression. From the drip paintings of Jackson Pollock to the frenetic portraits of Willem de Kooning, the art world was bursting with the wild lines and bold hues of Abstract Expressionism.

Although many Americans didn't immediately embrace this new art movement, often dismissing it as unskilled or simply weird and ugly, they did warm to its aesthetic. Taking a cue from the action painters of the world, many designers began incorporating the Abstract Expressionist look into their work. Products from appliances to textiles reflected the feel of a Franz Kline painting.

OKM's Elizabeth Foderaro was among the many commercial artists happy to infuse their work with fresh new influences. She translated the dense concepts of the art world into beautiful, wearable pieces, like the Abstract Expressionist. Foderaro treated the sweater as a blank canvas, with a plain white body, and then created a separate offset graphic that was hand-sewn onto it. The result is a sweater that feels very much like a work of art, its dynamic layering of colors reminiscent of a Miró.

The original Abstract Expressionist sweater was likely designed for the Eastmoor Company, a California-based label that specialized in high-fashion designs at more affordable prices. Considering the sophistication of the style and the additional hand finishing, this would have been a pricier item for the Ohio Knitting Mills to create.

This very basic sweater body serves as a canvas for the playful embroidered pattern. Use the original 1950s design provided here, or let out your own inner Abstract Expressionist!

SIZES

To fit bust 30 (34, 38, 42, 46) inches

FINISHED MEASUREMENTS

Bust 32 (35¾, 40½, 44¼, 48) inches
Length 21½ (22, 23, 23½, 24½) inches

YARN

Lion Brand Fishermen's Wool (100% wool;
465 yds per 227 g)
MC: #150-098 Natural, 2 (2, 3, 3, 3) skeins

Lion Brand Vanna's Choice (100% acrylic;
170 yds per 100 g)
1 skein each of:
CC1: #860-180 Cranberry
CC2: #860-141 Wild Berry
CC3: #860-174 Olive
CC4: #860-170 Pea Green
Note that only a small amount of each color
is needed for the embroidery. This is a good
opportunity to use oddments of yarn from
your stash.

NEEDLES

U.S. size 4 (3.5 mm) straight needles
U.S. size 4 (3.5 mm) circular needle,
16 inches long
U.S. size 3 (3.25 mm) straight needles
U.S. size 3 (3.25 mm) circular needle,
16 inches long
Adjust needle sizes as needed to obtain gauge.

NOTIONS

Stitch holder
Tapestry needle
Dressmaker's tracing transfer paper (available
at quilting and sewing stores)

GAUGE

21 sts and 29 rows = 4 inches/10 cm in St st
on larger needles

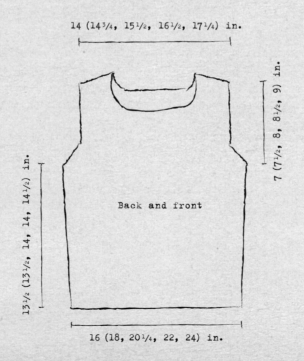

14 (14¾, 15½, 16½, 17¼) in.

7 (7½, 8, 8½, 9) in.

13½ (13½, 14, 14, 14½) in.

Back and front

16 (18, 20¼, 22, 24) in.

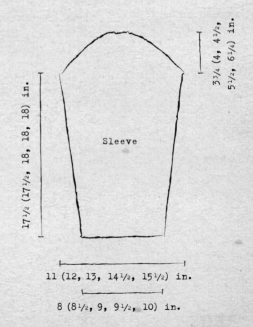

3¾ (4, 4½, 5½, 6¼) in.

17½ (17½, 18, 18, 18) in.

Sleeve

11 (12, 13, 14½, 15½) in.

8 (8½, 9, 9½, 10) in.

BACK

With smaller straight needles and MC, cast on 80 (90, 102, 112, 122) sts. Work k1, p1 rib for 10 rows. Change to larger needles and continue in St st for 25 rows, ending with WS row. Inc 1 st at each end of next row, then every following 26th row twice more—86 (96, 108, 118, 128) sts. Work even until piece measures 13½ (13½, 14, 14, 14½) inches from cast-on edge, ending with a WS row.

Shape Armhole

Sizes 30 (34, 38) Only

Dec 1 st at each end of every RS row until 76 (80, 84) sts rem.**

Sizes 42 (46) Only

Dec 1 st at each end of every row 10 times, then every RS row until 88 (92) sts rem.**

All Sizes

Work even until armholes measure 6½ (7, 7½, 8, 8½) inches, ending with a WS row.

Shape Neck and Shoulders

Next row (RS): k26 (27, 28, 29, 30); turn work, placing rem sts on holder.

Working right shoulder only:

Row 1 (WS): Bind off 3 sts, p to end.

Row 2 (RS): Knit.

Row 3: Bind off 3 sts, p to end—20 (21, 22, 23, 24) sts rem.

Row 4: Bind off 5 (5, 5, 5, 6) sts, k to last 2 sts, k2tog.

Row 5: Purl.

Row 6: Bind off 4 (5, 5, 5, 5) sts, k to last 2 sts, k2tog.

Row 7: Purl.

Row 8: Bind off 4 (4, 5, 5, 5) sts, k to last 2 sts, k2tog.

Row 9: Purl.

Row 10: Bind off rem 4 (4, 4, 5, 5) sts.

Join yarn to held sts with RS facing and bind off 24 (26, 28, 30, 32) sts for back neck. Complete left shoulder to match right side, reversing shaping.

FRONT

Work same as Back to **.

Work even until armholes measure 5½ (6, 6½, 7, 7½) inches, ending with a WS row.

Shape Neck and Shoulders

Next row (RS): k32 (33, 34, 35, 36); turn work, placing rem sts on holder.

Working left shoulder only:

Row 1 (WS): Bind off 6 sts, p to end.

Row 2 (RS): Knit to last 2 sts, k2tog.

Row 3: p2tog, p to end—24 (25, 26, 27, 28) sts rem.

Continue to dec 1 st at neck edge each row until 17 (18, 19, 20, 21) sts rem.

Work even, if necessary, until armhole measures 7 (7½, 8, 8½, 9) inches, ending with a WS row.

Next row (RS): Bind off 5 (5, 5, 5, 6) sts, k to end.

Next row: Purl.

Next row: Bind off 4 (5, 5, 5, 5) sts, k to end.

Next row: Purl.

Next row: Bind off 4 (4, 5, 5, 5) sts, k to end.

Next row: Purl.

Next row: Bind off rem 4 (4, 4, 5, 5) sts.

Join yarn to held sts with RS facing and bind off 12 (14, 16, 18, 20) sts for front neck. Complete right shoulder to match left side, reversing shaping.

SLEEVES

With smaller needles and MC, cast on 44 (46, 50, 52, 54) sts. Work k1, p1 rib for 10 rows.

Change to larger needles and continue in St st for 7 rows, ending with WS row. Inc 1 st at each end of next row, then every following 10th (8th, 8th, 8th, 6th) row to 60 (64, 70, 78, 84) sts. Work even until piece measures 17½ (17½, 18, 18, 18) inches from cast-on edge, ending with a WS row.

Shape Cap

Bind off 2 sts at beg of next 2 rows.

Dec 1 st at each end of next 7 (7, 10, 9, 10) rows, then on RS rows only 5 (6, 6, 8, 11) times, then every row until 12 sts rem.

Bind off.

FINISHING

Block pieces.

Embroidery

Note: The embroidery is meant to be abstract. Depending on your skill level, it may not be necessary to transfer every single line of the embroidery template.

Prepare the Template

Using a photocopy machine and the Abstract Expressionist embroidery template on page 73, enlarge the template so that the height of the motif fits into the center front of the sweater above the ribbing. A copy shop can assist you.

Transfer the Template

Note: Use dressmaker's tracing paper in a shade that will show up on the knitted fabric.

Lay the sweater Front flat on a hard surface. Place the tracing paper beneath the enlarged template and lay them on the sweater above the ribbing. The template should be placed so that its left edge is at the right edge of the knitted piece. Pin through both layers to attach them to the sweater. Using a ballpoint pen, trace right on top of the design, pressing so that the design transfers to the sweater.

Embroider Pattern

Note: Use a single strand of yarn throughout.

All of the embroidery is worked in Running st with the exception of the five-pointed leaf motifs on the right side of the template, which are worked in Chain st.

The Running st is not a traditional Running st: most of the yarn should float on the right side of the fabric. To do this, take very small pick stitches through only one ply of the knitted surface. The embroidery yarn will barely be visible on the back of the pieces. This will make the embroidered lines rest on the top of the fabric.

Beginning with the center motif, work the center line, referring to the template and photo. This will give you a base to work the rest of the motif around.

Work the diamond motif, placing the lines of Running st very close together to give a filled-in appearance.

Work the swooping lines in Running st on either side of the diamond motif, following the template and the photograph.

Complete the embroidery by working the five-pointed leaf motifs in Chain st.

Collar

Sew shoulder seams. With MC and RS facing, using smaller circular needle and beg at left shoulder seam, pick up and knit 3 sts for every 4 rows and 1 st in every bound-off st around neckline, ending with a multiple of 2 sts. Work 10 rounds of k1, p1 rib. Change to larger circular needle and work rib for 20 more rounds. Bind off loosely in patt.

Set in sleeves. Sew side and sleeve seams. Weave in ends.

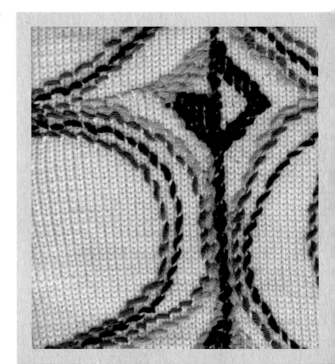

Cranberry

Wild Berry

Olive

Pea Green

Bottom

OHIO KNITTING MILLS
Original Design

Fall   1958

4701 PERKINS AVENUE
CLEVELAND, O. 44103

Beatnik Babe

Not everyone in 1950s America was busy having babies and vacuuming wall-to-wall carpeting. Just as teenagers had developed their own subculture, older antiestablishment types who found the *The Donna Reed Show* lifestyle constricting and superficial developed their own enclaves of subversive style. This was the birth of cool.

Hipsters, unimpressed by the conformity of all the new subdivisions in the suburbs, swarmed to major urban areas such as San Francisco and New York. These intellectual types, sporting goatees and sunglasses and tossing around a jive-influenced jargon, gathered at bookstores for beat poetry readings, smoky nightclubs for the bebop sounds of Charlie Parker, and art galleries for the latest works from Robert Rauschenberg and Jasper Johns. In 1958 the Pulitzer Prize–winning journalist Herb Caen called these low-key arty types "beatniks," popularizing Jack Kerouac's 1948 proclamation that he was part of the "beat generation."

For the most part, the beats remained underground, recluses as much kin to thieves and drug pushers as to art dealers and publishing houses. But it wasn't long before the nuances of this subculture came to the surface and were mimicked and appropriated by the mainstream—influencing the fashion choices of the very homemakers this subculture disdained.

While the Beatnik Babe would have belonged at a Greenwich Village jazz club, it blended in just as well at a picnic with the kids. Again, OKM designer Elizabeth Foderaro looked toward the cool set to influence her work—from the three-quarter-length sleeves and boatneck design to the saturated hues of the Mark Rothko–influenced fabric.

Sweaters like the Beatnik Babe made the "new cool" of an elite subculture available to Middle America, which was just as eager to be in the forefront of fashion. For $16.99, sophistication could be bought at any department store or small-town boutique.

Today this sweater looks as fresh as the day it was designed—a dynamic addition to any fashionista's closet. Worn with a pair of black leggings and ballerina flats, it'll make any girl look like a tried and true beat.

Just three colors, nothing fancy, and very manageable for an intermediate knitter—but such a hip result! We've replicated the textured effect of the original yarns by using a thick-and-thin handspun.

SIZES
To fit bust 30 (34, 38, 42, 46) inches

FINISHED MEASUREMENTS
Bust 32½ (36¾, 41, 45½, 48½) inches
Length 21½ (22, 23, 23½, 24) inches

YARN
Manos del Uruguay Wool Clásica (100% wool; 137 yds per 100 g)
A: #68 Citric (yellow-green), 3 (3, 4, 4, 5) skeins
B: #Q Calypso (blue), 3 (3, 4, 4, 5) skeins
C: #8 Black, 1 skein

Any smooth worsted weight yarn (for facings, hems, and seaming), approximately 50 yds each, blue and green to match

NEEDLES
U.S. size 8 (5 mm) straight needles
U.S. size 7 (4.5 mm) straight needles
Adjust needle sizes as needed to obtain gauge.

NOTIONS
Tapestry needle
Needle and thread

GAUGE
15 sts and 22 rows = 4 inches/10 cm in St st on larger needles

NOTES
When measuring length of pieces, do not include the hems (those portions worked in the worsted weight yarn).

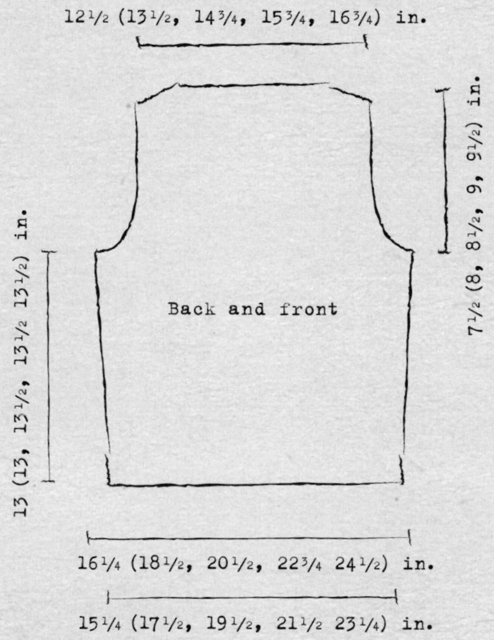
12½ (13½, 14¾, 15¾, 16¾) in.
7½ (8, 8½, 9, 9½) in.
Back and front
13 (13, 13½, 13½ 13½) in.
16¼ (18½, 20½, 22¾ 24½) in.
15¼ (17½, 19½, 21½ 23¼) in.

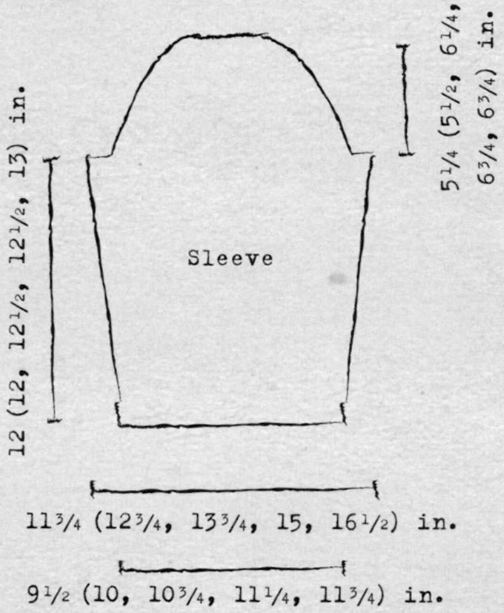
5¼ (5½, 6¼, 6¾, 6¾) in.
Sleeve
12 (12, 12½, 12½, 13) in.
11¾ (12¾, 13¾, 15, 16½) in.
9½ (10, 10¾, 11¼, 11¾) in.

BACK

With smaller needles and either color worsted weight yarn, cast on 59 (67, 75, 83, 89) sts. Work in St st for 1 inch, ending with a RS row. Cut yarn.

Setup row 1 (WS): p28 (32, 36, 40, 43) in A; p3 in C; p28 (32, 36, 40, 43) in B.

Setup row 2: k28 (32, 36, 40, 43) in B; k3 in C; k28 (32, 36, 40, 43) in A. Maintain this color arrangement throughout.

Work even as established for 2 inches, ending with a WS row.

Change to larger needles.

Work 20 rows even.

Inc row (RS): k2, m1, knit to last 2 sts, m1, k2—61 (69, 77, 85, 91) sts total.

Work 21 rows even.

Rep Inc row—63 (71, 79, 87, 93) sts total.

Work even until piece measures 13 (13, 13½, 13½, 13½) inches, ending with a WS row.

Shape Armholes

Bind off 4 (4, 5, 5, 6) sts at beg of next 2 rows—55 (63, 69, 77, 81) sts rem.

Work 2 rows even.

Dec 1 st at each end of next row and every following 4th (4th, 2nd, 2nd, 2nd) row until 49 (53, 57, 61, 65) sts rem.

Work even until armholes measure 7½ (8, 8½, 9, 9½) inches, ending with a WS row.

Shape Shoulders and Neck

Rows 1 and 2: Work to last 3 (3, 3, 4, 4) sts, wrap and turn.

Rows 3 and 4: Work to last 6 (6, 6, 8, 8) sts, wrap and turn.

Rows 5 and 6: Work to last 9 (10, 11, 12, 13) sts, wrap and turn.

Row 7 (RS): Knit to end, hiding wraps.

Row 8: Bind off 10 (11, 12, 13, 14) sts, p to last 10 (11, 12, 13, 14) sts, bind off last 10 (11, 12, 13, 14) sts, hiding wraps.

Join either color worsted weight yarn to rem 29 (31, 33, 35, 37) sts with WS facing. With smaller needles, work in St st on these sts for 1 inch, inc 1 st at each end of every row. Bind off.

FRONT

Work same as Back, except set up colors as follows:

Setup row 1 (WS): p28 (32, 36, 40, 43) in B; p3 in C; p28 (32, 36, 40, 43) in A.

Setup row 2 (RS): k28 (32, 36, 40, 43) in A; k3 in C; k28 (32, 36, 40, 43) in B. Maintain this color arrangement throughout.

SLEEVES

Make 1 sleeve in A and 1 sleeve in B. Use coordinating worsted weight yarn for hems.

With smaller needles and worsted weight yarn, cast on 38 (40, 42, 44, 46) sts. Work in St st for 1 inch, ending with a RS row. Change to A or B and work 1 inch even in St st, ending with a WS row.

Change to larger needles.

Work 8 rows even.

Inc row (RS): k2, m1, knit to last 2 sts, m1, k2—40 (42, 44, 46, 48) sts.

Rep Inc row on every following 10th (10th, 8th, 8th, 6th) row to 46 (50, 54, 58, 64) sts.

Work even until sleeve measures 12 (12, 12½, 12½, 13) inches, ending with a WS row.

Shape Cap

Bind off 4 (4, 5, 5, 6) sts at beg of next 2 rows—38 (42, 44, 48, 52) sts rem.

Dec 1 st at each end of next row and following 3 (5, 5, 7, 8) RS rows, then every 4th row 3 (2, 3, 2, 0) times, then every RS row to 16 sts.

Work 1 WS row even.

Bind off 2 sts at beg of next 2 rows.

Bind off rem 12 sts.

FINISHING

Use worsted weight yarn for all seaming.

Block pieces. Seam shoulders and neck facings. Turn facing to inside and slip-stitch in place, taking care not to let sts show through on RS of sweater.

Set sleeves into armholes. Sew side and sleeve seams, including hems. Turn hems to inside and slip-stitch in place as for neck facing. Weave in ends. Steam hems and neck facing to flatten.

OHIO KNITTING MILLS
Original Design

Fall   1952

4701 PERKINS AVENUE
CLEVELAND, O. 44103

The All-American

Thanks to the GI Bill, signed into law in 1944, World War II veterans, and eventually an even larger number of Korean War vets, were able to head off to college, where they traded in their uniforms and rifles for football helmets and megaphones.

The 1950s was entirely sports-crazed, most iconically represented by Saturday afternoon gridiron battles, guys clad in school colors, cheerleaders, and team pennants. Sports, particularly in high school and college, had become one more outlet for America to play out its competitive fervor, patriotic pride, and aim for excellence.

The Ohio Knitting Mills found itself with a swarm of customers looking for clothes that were collegiate and athletic—an aesthetic that combined a bright-eyed conviction with a robust and hardworking ethos that described the U.S.A. Whether on the field or in the bleachers, everyone was on the team in his All-American.

Made of 100 percent virgin wool in a thick gauge, The All-American embodied reliability. A quintessential piece for a crisp fall scrimmage or studying by the fire, it gave any guy just the right amount of brawn.

It's no wonder that The All-American is one of OKM's all-time best sellers. It was originally developed for Campus Sportswear Company, a Cleveland-based label that was one of the Mills' biggest customers at the time. Campus Sportswear had long been dressing men and boys for work and play in practical and traditional pieces, from cardigans to letterman jackets. By the 1950s the label had cemented its reputation for sturdy, strapping designs and clean-cut, versatile separates.

Not only did The All-American suit the 1950s appetite for team spirit and love of leisure, it also provided a fashionable transition for teenagers who were trading in their hot rods and bobby socks for dorm rooms and scholarly pursuits.

This sporty number is knit cuff to cuff and in dolman style. The black-white combo is striking, but substitute your old college colors instead for cheering on your team at the big game.

SIZES
Men's S/M (L/XL)

FINISHED MEASUREMENTS
Chest 39 (44) inches
Length 25 (27) inches

YARN
Cascade Yarns Cascade 220
(100% wool; 220 yds per 100 g)
#8555 Black, 5 (6) skeins
#8010 Natural, 3 (3) skeins

NEEDLES
U.S. size 7 (4.5 mm) circular needle,
24 inches or longer
U.S. size 5 (3.75 mm) circular needle,
24 inches long
Adjust needle sizes as needed to obtain gauge.

NOTIONS
Row counter
Tapestry needle
Three ¾-inch buttons
Needle and thread

GAUGE
22 sts and 24 rows = 4 inches/10 cm in k1, p1 rib on larger needles, blocked

NOTES
Knit in two pieces (back and front), cuff to cuff, seamed at underarms and top of arms/shoulders. Worked entirely in k1, p1 rib.
In a dolman sweater, the line where the sleeves end and the body begins is indeterminate, so there is more room around the chest under the arms than the figures indicate. The larger size will fit a man up to about 44 inches around the chest.

STITCH INSTRUCTIONS
Stripe Pattern Size S/M
7 rows natural, 16 rows black, *8 rows natural, 16 rows black; rep from *, end with 7 rows natural.

Stripe Pattern Size L/XL
7 rows black, *10 rows natural, 18 rows black; rep from *, end with 7 rows black.

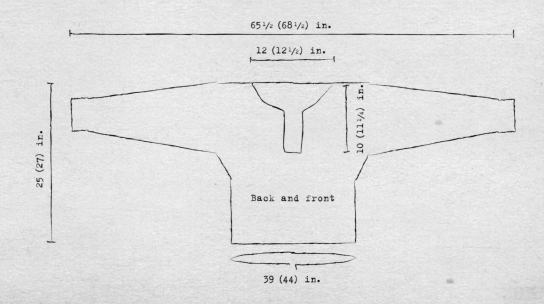

65½ (68½) in.

12 (12½) in.

10 (11¼) in.

25 (27) in.

Back and front

39 (44) in.

BACK

Begin at left cuff. With smaller needles and black, cast on 30 (32) sts. Work 2 inches in k1, p1 rib.

Sleeve/Dolman Shaping

Change to larger needles and begin working Stripe patt. Inc 1 st at each end of every 8th row (RS) 10 (9) times, then every 4th row 5 (7) times, then every 2nd row 5 (6) times. Cast on 2 sts at beg of next 4 RS rows—78 (84) sts total.

Cast on 8 sts at beg of next 2 RS rows, then cast on 34 (36) sts at beg of next RS row—128 (136) sts total and 124 (126) rows from cuff.**

Body

Work even for 117 (135) rows—241 (261) rows from cuff in total.

Dolman Shaping/Sleeve

***Bind off 34 (36) sts at beg of next RS row, then bind off 8 sts at beg of next 2 RS rows—78 (84) sts rem.

Bind off 2 sts at beg of next 4 RS rows.

Dec 1 st at each end of every 2nd row 6 (7) times, then every 4th row 5 (7) times, then every 8th row 9 (8) times—30 (32) sts rem.

Work 8 rows even—366 (388) rows from cuff in total.

Change to smaller needles and work k1, p1 rib in black for 2 inches. Bind off.

FRONT

Begin at left cuff. Work as for Back to **.

Body

Work even for 23 (31) rows—147 (157) rows from cuff in total.

Neck Shaping

Next row (RS): Bind off 9 (11) sts, work to end.

Dec 1 st at beg of next 13 RS rows. Work 1 row even. You should be at the end of a natural stripe, about to begin a black stripe.

Next row (RS): With black, bind off 34 (38) sts, work to end—72 (74) sts rem.

Work 15 (17) rows even. You should be at the end of the black stripe, about to begin a natural stripe.

Next row (RS): Cast on 34 (38) sts with black. Change to natural and work to end.

Work 1 row even.

Inc 1 st at beg of next 13 RS rows.

Next RS row: Cast on 9 (11) sts, work to end—128 (136) sts.

Work even for 22 (30) rows—244 (262) rows from cuff in total.

Dolman Shaping/Sleeve

Complete as for Back from ***, reversing shaping by binding off at the beg of WS rows.

FINISHING

Bottom Ribbings

With smaller needles, black, and RS facing, pick up and knit 96 (108) sts from bottom edge of body on Front. Work k1, p1 rib for 2¼ inches. Bind off. Repeat on Back.

Block.

Seam Front and Back together at overarm and underarm/side seam

Collar

With smaller needles, black, and RS facing, beg at right side of Front placket opening, pick up and knit 3 sts for every 4 rows and 1 st for every cast-on or bound-off stitch along placket edge, around neckline, and down left side of placket opening. Work in k1, p1 rib for 1 inch. Mark positions for 3 buttonholes on left side. On next row, make buttonholes at marked positions by binding off 3 sts at each place, then on next row casting on 3 sts over gaps, using the backward loop method. Work in rib until collar measures 2 (2¼) inches. Bind off. Attach buttons. Slip-stitch free bottom edges of collar in place. Steam collar lightly; do not flatten rib.

PROJECTS IN THIS CHAPTER

The 1960s

BRIGHT, BOLD, AND BOHEMIAN

From civil rights to psychedelia, 1960s America was bursting with major social changes. The traditionalism of the fifties was being challenged on numerous fronts, most notably by the struggle for racial equality and, as the decade progressed, by a growing opposition to the Vietnam War. These polarizing events helped propel America into cultural chaos, giving birth to a range of new social tribes, including bikers, folkies, and hippies.

As the beats and modernist artists had rejected the quaint orthodoxy of the 1950s, young adults in the new decade questioned and abandoned the rigid protocols of their parents. From antiwar protests and sit-ins to the sexual revolution and drug-fueled happenings, the sixties generation exploded with experimentation and rapid change. It was the end of the Wild West and the rise of surf culture, non-Western religions, and communal living.

Meanwhile, business for the Ohio Knitting Mills was better than ever. All these new lifestyles also required new modes of dressing—like hip-hugging shifts and easygoing pullovers.

Designer Elizabeth Foderaro kept a constant eye on the revolving trends of the times, taking cues from both suburban homemakers and rambling hippies alike. If America wanted its skirts short, she'd go shorter, and if it wanted its sweaters brighter, she'd go even bolder.

Part of the Ohio Knitting Mills' great success during the 1960s had to do with the company's age-old warp knitting machines. These machines had been operating at the Mills since the company's inception in 1927, but it was the bold new looks of the sixties that allowed the machines to really work their magic. The warp machine's ability to layer color upon color and texture upon texture is unparalleled. It was the perfect method for quickly producing large quantities of textiles with the dynamic and bold variegated patterns that were in such high demand.

America during the 1960s was a vibrant and chaotic stew of progressive social movements and colorful cultural happenings. And for the Ohio Knitting Mills, this decade gave birth to its most iconic and creative work yet.

OHIO KNITTING MILLS
Original Design

Fall _____ 19 68

4701 PERKINS AVENUE
CLEVELAND, O. 44103

The Wavy Gravy

Walter Cronkite announced that America was heading to space on the *CBS Evening News;* the soul-stirring backbeat of the Temptations, the Supremes, and other black recording artists crossed over onto traditionally white radio stations; and an advertising illustrator from Pittsburgh named Andy Warhol took the art world by storm with bright, bold pieces mimicking Campbell's soup cans and Brillo boxes.

Meanwhile, the Ohio Knitting Mills was at its peak of production, its machines cranking out colorful and timely fabrics like those in The Wavy Gravy, a pattern that perfectly expresses the vibrant spirit of its times.

Chunky lines of bold colors oscillate up and down the sweater's boxy shape. Worn with a mod mini, thick tights, and flats, it would have made many a small-town girl feel absolutely chic.

Elizabeth Foderaro designed the TV-test-pattern fabric for Jack Winter, a knitwear magnate out of Wisconsin who made his fortune from women's stretch pants and reinvested his riches in bringing the Brewers baseball team to Milwaukee. Winter embraced the pop fashion aesthetic; some of OKM's most garish color schemes and craziest patterns were developed just for Jack Winter's line of sportswear.

Taking a cue from America's amusement with exploration—from the dark mystery of outer space to the inner recesses of our minds—Foderaro was busy translating America's cultural explosion into exuberant new fabrics bursting with cheerful hues. The Wavy Gravy's cartoonishly chunky knit, loose cowl-neck, and hypnotic color scheme was the perfect garb for a world rediscovering itself and appealed to the sensibilities of both housewives and emerging hippies. The textile for The Wavy Gravy was so popular it was translated into many other pieces—from vests and cardigans to pullovers and ponchos.

Another classic mid-century OKM sweater: the high, wide collar, short body, and wild colors are quintessential sixties. We've reinterpreted the thick texture of the original Raschel knit as a Stockinette stitch body with double-thick Chain stitch embroidery.

SIZES
To fit bust 30 (34, 38, 42, 46) inches

FINISHED MEASUREMENTS
Bust 30 (34, 38, 42, 46) inches
Length 21¼ (21¾, 22¼, 23¼, 23¾) inches

YARN
Cascade Yarns Cascade 220 (100% wool; 220 yds per 100 g)
MC: #8555 Black, 4 (5, 5, 6, 6) skeins

Classic Elite Montera (50% llama, 50% wool; 127 yds per 100 g)
1 skein each of:
#3810 Necropolis Navy
#3856 Majolica Blue
#3852 Peruvian Potato
#3827 Cochineal
#3885 Bolsita Orange
#3858 Cintachi Red
#3836 Straw
#3840 Tuscan Hills
#3843 Coffee Bean

NEEDLES
U.S. size 7 (4.5 mm) circular needle, 24 inches long
Set of U.S. size 7 (4.5 mm) double-pointed needles
Adjust needle sizes as needed to obtain gauge.

NOTIONS
Stitch holder
Stitch markers
Tapestry needle
U.S. size I (5.5 mm) crochet hook
Pins

GAUGE
20 sts and 28 rows = 4 inches/10 cm in St st

NOTES
Body and sleeves are knit in the round to the armholes, then flat to the shoulder.

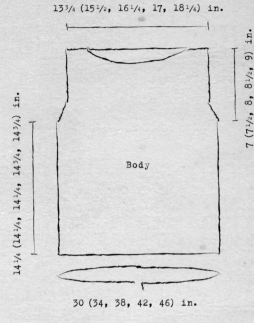

13¾ (15½, 16¼, 17, 18¼) in.

7 (7½, 8, 8½, 9) in.

14¼ (14¼, 14¼, 14¾, 14¾) in.

Body

30 (34, 38, 42, 46) in.

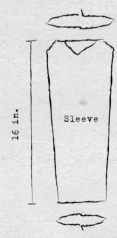

13¾ (14¼, 15, 15¾, 16½) in.

16 in.

Sleeve

10½ (11, 11½, 11¾, 12¼) in.

BODY

With MC and circular needle, cast on 150 (170, 190, 210, 230) sts. Place marker and join to work in the round. Work in St st for 14¼ (14¼, 14¼, 14¾, 14¾) inches.

Divide Back and Front

Next rnd: k75 (85, 95, 105, 115), turn.

Place rem sts on holder.

Upper Back

Row 1 (WS): Purl to end.

Dec 1 st at each end of next row and every following RS row until 71 (79, 83, 87, 93) sts rem. Work even until armholes measure 7 (7½, 8, 8½, 9) inches. Bind off.

Upper Front

Join yarn to sts on holder with RS facing. Knit 1 row. Purl 1 row.

Dec 1 st at each end of next row and every following RS row until 71 (79, 83, 87, 93) sts rem. Work even until armholes measure 6 (6½, 7, 7½, 8) inches, ending with a WS row.

Shape Neck

Next row (RS): k13 (14, 16, 18, 20), join a second ball of MC yarn and bind off center 45 (51, 51, 51, 53) sts, k to end.

Working both sides at the same time, dec 1 st at each neck edge on next 5 rows. Work 1 row even.

Bind off.

COLLAR

Seam shoulders.

With WS facing and MC, pick up and knit 55 (61, 61, 61, 63) sts across back neckline, pm, pick up and knit 57 (63, 63, 63, 65) sts across front neckline. Place marker and join to work in the round. Work in St st, inc 1 st on either side of each marker on every 2nd rnd (4 sts increased every 2nd rnd). When collar measures 4 inches, bind off.

SLEEVES

With MC and dpn, cast on 53 (55, 57, 59, 61) sts. Place marker and join to work in the round. Work in St st, inc 1 st at beg and end of every 8th rnd until there are 69 (71, 75, 79, 83) sts on the needles. Work even until sleeve measures 16 inches, or desired length to underarm.

Shape Cap

Cap is worked back and forth in rows.

Purl 1 WS row.

Dec 1 st at each end of next row, and every following RS row until there are 65 (65, 63, 61, 61) sts on the needle.

Bind off.

FINISHING

Embroidery

Note: The embroidery is done in a free-form, undulating design, using a double strand of each color throughout.

Sweater Front

Determine the center of the sweater front and mark the center stitch with a pin. With pins, stitch markers, or a basting stitch, mark the center stitch up the entire center front. This line will act as the guide for embroidery stitching.

Beginning at center front, work a wavy line of Chain stitch up the center front of the sweater (refer to the photograph on page 88), using a double strand of yarn. The line should move to the left ½ inch, then back to the center front, and then to the right ½ inch. There should be a total of five waves: * to the left, back to the right ½ inch past the center line; * rep once more, then back to the left. The first embroidered wavy line will become the basis for the remainder of the embroidery. Each Chain stitch should be approximately ½ inch long.

Work a second line of Chain stitch in the same color, placing it 1¼ inches to the right of the first line of embroidery and following the wave pattern established.

Switch to the next color yarn. Work a line of Chain stitch, placing it 1½ inches from the second line of embroidery, and follow the wave pattern established. Then work a second line of Chain stitch in the same color, placing it 1¼ inches to the right of the line just completed. Note that the gap between lines of the same color will be smaller than the gap between lines of different colors.

Continue the wave pattern with the remaining colors until you have 9 pairs of wavy lines, as shown in the photo.

Collar

Continue the wave embroidery at the collar. The collar folds over, so make sure the line of Chain stitch is placed on the correct side of the collar fabric.

Sleeves

Work the same as the body of the sweater. Determine center of sleeve and place embroidery the same as on body. Because of the sleeve shape, the wave motif will be shorter as you reach the underarm.

Assembly

Set sleeves into armholes.

Weave in ends and block.

With any CC (we used Necropolis Navy) and crochet hook, work 2 rnds of single crochet around bottom edge of sweater and edge of collar. Work 4 rnds of single crochet around cuffs.

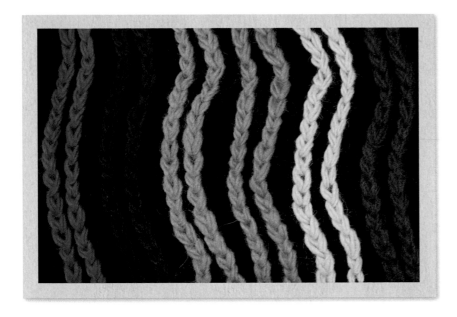

THE WOMEN OF OHIO KNITTING MILLS

Theresa Yacabucci was only seventeen years old when Walker Woodworth gave her work on the factory floor of the Stone Knitting Mills.

It was 1930 and the Depression had left once prosperous men out on the streets, peddling apples on street corners. Theresa was the oldest of six children, the doe-eyed daughter of Italian immigrants. Her mother had passed away, and her father's steel mill wages weren't enough to sustain the family through such hard times. After she graduated from middle school, her father told Theresa she'd have to forgo high school and get a job to help support the family.

Theresa Yacabucci at seventeen.

Having heard the Stone Knitting Mills might be hiring, Theresa started getting up early every weekday and taking a bus to the National Screw building on Stanton Avenue. Finally, one morning Walker pulled her out of the desperate crowd of unemployed men and women and sent her to work in the trimming department; her pay was thirty-five cents an hour.

Theresa loved working at Stone so much that she never left. Even when Leonard Rand took over the company, she stayed. Theresa, who never married and is (as of this writing) alive and well at the age of ninety-six, describes the mill as her home away from home. She attended her coworkers' weddings and birthdays, as well as the christenings of their children.

One employee Theresa remembers well is Agnes Harichovszky, who fled Hungary after Soviet troops crushed the 1956 revolt. Once Agnes and her husband made it from a refugee camp in Austria to Cleveland, she started working in the OKM trimming department, reporting to Theresa. "She was a good worker," Theresa says of Agnes. "And good workers were hard to come by."

Leonard Rand was quickly impressed by Agnes's organizational skills, so he promoted her to the purchasing and planning department ("I was mad when they moved her," Theresa admits). There, Agnes was in charge of all of the incoming orders, from Montgomery Ward to small mom-and-pop stores. Like Theresa, Agnes made the Ohio Knitting Mills her home away from home. She became Leonard Rand's right-hand woman and served as Gary Rand's mentor. While Theresa retired in 1993, after a sixty-three-year-long career, Agnes stayed on with the company until 2005.

It was hardworking, talented, and unfailing women like Agnes and Theresa who were the heart and soul of Ohio Knitting Mills, keeping the Mills going, churning out millions of sweaters for more than seventy-five years.

OHIO KNITTING MILLS
Original Design

Spring 19 66

4701 PERKINS AVENUE
CLEVELAND, O. 44103

Go-Go Girl

From Betty Friedan and Nancy Sinatra to housewives and their teenage daughters, women of the 1960s were exploring their sexuality and all of its facets. They were shortening their skirts and claiming a new version of womanhood, one that celebrated their intellect and sovereignty, as well as their physical beauty and personal strength. The clothing of the era reflected this shift, emphasizing—rather than restricting—the female form.

When the birth control pill was approved for sale in the United States in 1960, it was a seismic shift. This easy, reliable contraceptive meant that more women felt free to be sexually active without worrying about the possibility of pregnancy. The introduction of the Pill was perhaps the key catalyst jump-starting the sexual revolution, which began in hip enclaves like San Francisco and London and then spread over the Western world as the decade progressed. And with it came a new free wheeling aesthetic. Icons like Twiggy pranced around the pages of fashion magazines in more eye makeup

than clothing. As hemlines receded, boots got taller and eyelashes grew longer. Even Middle America was entranced by the groovy new styles, evident by the popularity of this sassy OKM original: the Go-Go Girl.

Always a leader in trends, OKM had been paying close attention to the fashion coming out of Europe. So when the Brits went short, designer Elizabeth Foderaro did too—and for a lot less money—bringing what was in vogue to Main Street America.

Also inspired by the mini shifts worn by Warhol starlet Edie Sedgwick, Foderaro created this edgy yet simple cut-and-sew pattern, meaning that the dresses could simply be cut from a giant roll of knitted fabric and then quickly pieced together by the Mills' arsenal of sewing machines. Form-fitting and short enough to hit mid-thigh, the piece was a perfect expression of its time. Its basic shape worked well as a canvas for myriad colorful and creative yarns, the foundation of the OKM look.

Our updated version of the tunic in horizontal stripes features brushed mohair, giving it a soft and shimmering surface, and a removable waist tie. Designed to be the fashion soul mate of killer knee-high boots, more than forty years later this dress still promises to turn heads.

SIZES
To fit bust 30 (34, 38, 42, 46) inches

FINISHED MEASUREMENTS
Bust 30 (34, 38½, 42½, 46) inches
Length 30 (30½, 31, 31½, 32) inches

YARN
Classic Elite Princess (40% merino wool, 28% viscose, 10% cashmere, 7% angora, 15% nylon; 150 yds per 50 g)
MC: #3427 Côtes du Rhône, 4 (4, 6, 6, 7) skeins

Classic Elite La Gran (76½% mohair, 17½% wool, 6% nylon; 90 yds per 42 g)
A: #6555 Infra Red, 2 (2, 3, 3, 3) skeins
B: #6527 Chinese Red, 2 (2, 3, 3, 3) skeins
C: #63588 Peach Blossom, 2 (2, 3, 3, 3) skeins
D: #6540 Honeydew, 2 (2, 3, 3, 3) skeins

NEEDLES
U.S. size 7 (4.5 mm) straight needles
Adjust needle size as needed to obtain gauge.

NOTIONS
Tapestry needle
Metal rings
1½–2 yds cording
Needle and thread

GAUGE
15 sts and 19 rows = 4 inches/10 cm in St st

NOTES
The MC yarn is used double-stranded throughout the pattern, while yarns A, B, C, and D are used single-stranded.

STITCH INSTRUCTIONS
Stripe Pattern
*4 rows in A; 2 rows in MC; 4 rows in B; 2 rows in MC; 4 rows in C; 2 rows in MC; 4 rows in D; 2 rows in MC; rep from *.

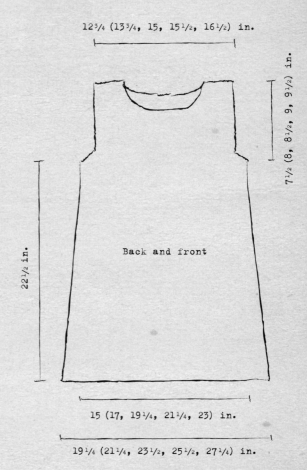

12¾ (13¾, 15, 15½, 16½) in.

7½ (8, 8½, 9, 9½) in.

22½ in.

Back and front

15 (17, 19¼, 21¼, 23) in.

19¼ (21¼, 23½, 25½, 27¼) in.

BACK

With two strands of MC held together, cast on 80 (88, 96, 104, 110) sts. Knit 3 rows.

Begin working in St st with Stripe patt. Work 5 rows even, ending with RS facing.
Dec row (RS): k1, ssk, k to last 3 sts, k2tog, k1—78 (86, 94, 102, 108) sts rem.

Rep Dec row on every following 12th row until 70 (78, 86, 94, 100) sts rem. Work 5 rows even.

Bind off 3 sts at beg of next 2 rows to create side slit facings—64 (72, 80, 88, 94) sts rem.

Work 4 rows even.

Rep Dec row on next row and every following 12th row until 58 (66, 74, 82, 88) sts rem.

Work even until piece measures 22½ inches, ending with a WS row.

Shape Armhole

Row 1 (RS): k1, ssk, k to last 3 sts, k2tog, k1—56 (64, 72, 80, 86) sts rem.
Row 2 (WS): p1, p2tog, p to last 3 sts, p2tog tbl, p1.

Continue to dec on every row 1 (1, 3, 5, 7) times more, then on RS rows only until 48 (52, 56, 58, 62) sts rem.**

Work even until armholes measure 6 (6½, 7, 7½, 8) inches, ending with a WS row.

Shape Neck

Next row (RS): k15 (17, 17, 18, 19), join a second skein of yarn, bind off 18 (18, 22, 22, 24) sts for back neck, k15 (17, 17, 18, 19).

Working both sides at the same time with separate balls of yarn, dec 1 st at each neck edge on every row 6 times. Bind off rem 9 (11, 11, 12, 13) sts.

FRONT

Work same as Back to **.

Work even until armholes measure 4¾ (5¼, 5¾, 6¼, 6¾) inches, ending with a WS row.

Shape Neck

Next row (RS): k18 (20, 20, 21, 22), join a second skein of yarn, bind off 12 (12, 16, 16, 18) sts for front neck, k18 (20, 20, 21, 22).

Working both sides at the same time with separate balls of yarn, bind off 3 sts at each neck edge once. Dec 1 st at each neck edge on every row until 9 (11, 11, 12, 13) sts rem. Work 4 rows even, or until armholes measure same as Back to shoulder. Bind off.

FINISHING

Block gently.

Sew right shoulder seam.

With MC and RS facing, beg at left front shoulder, pick up and knit 2 sts for every 3 rows and 1 st in every bound-off st around neck. Knit 3 rows. Bind off.

Sew left shoulder and neck edging seam.

With MC and RS facing, beg at underarm, pick up and knit 2 sts for every 3 rows around armhole. Knit 3 rows. Bind off.

Sew side and armhole edging seams from armhole down to 3 bound-off sts. Fold the 3-st side slit facings to WS of tunic and slip-stitch in place.

Weave in ends. Sew metal rings, evenly spaced every 4 to 6 inches, around waist and string cord through for tie.

OHIO KNITTING MILLS
Original Design

Winter 19 64

4701 PERKINS AVENUE
CLEVELAND, O. 44103

Ski Chic Fatale

One can't mention the burgeoning sexuality of 1960s women without touching on the sexiest icon of them all—the Bond Girl.

Though writer Ian Fleming first created his dapper British spy in 1953, it wasn't until 1964, when a young Scottish actor by the name of Sean Connery appeared on the silver screen in *Goldfinger,* that Bond—James Bond—became a household name. (Two earlier Bond films had been modest hits, but this third in the series was a breakout smash.) Of course, Connery didn't make the 007 film franchise the most financially successful to date on his own. He had a little help from a string of sultry ladies who redefined what it meant to be a femme fatale in a world of feminism and free love.

From Honey Ryder to Pussy Galore, these Bond girls didn't just have beauty, but brains to boot. They were espionage experts, armed with bedroom eyes and just the right wardrobe—sneaky little pieces from barely-there bikinis to suggestive ski wear, such as this fast and furious number, the Ski Chic Fatale, which would have perfectly suited Tatiana Romanova in *From Russia with Love,* the second Bond film.

Ski sweaters had been one of OKM's best-selling products since the 1940s. These sweaters were modest, wholesome pieces—with precious designs of snowflakes and reindeer—that could easily be swapped between spouses or siblings for those family retreats to the mountains. But the Ski Chic Fatale changed all that.

By the early 1960s, OKM decided it was time to give its classic ski sweater a Bond Girl-worthy makeover. By simply cropping its length, adding an ultrafitted waist, and placing a long zipper down the front to accent the gently rolled turtleneck, Elizabeth Foderaro instantly made the ski sweater sexy, while still keeping its overall structure extremely practical.

This sweater offered women the edge they desired without sacrificing functionality. It's also a unique OKM design in that its style lies in the cut rather than the fabric itself, making it a relatively easy project for the home knitter.

The sporty shape with its high waist and generous armholes is easy to wear and quite warm, but still oh-so-stylish. The luxe alpaca-blend yarn knit in a loose and drapey Stockinette stitch elevates this piece from athletic wear to a versatile jacket.

SIZES
To fit bust 34 (38, 42, 46) inches

FINISHED MEASUREMENTS
Bust 38 (42, 45½, 50) inches
Length 18½ (18½, 19½, 19½) inches

YARN
Classic Elite Moorland (42% wool, 23% baby alpaca, 19% mohair, 16% acrylic; 147 yds per 50 g)
#2574 Abbey Stone, 11 (13, 14, 16) skeins

NEEDLES
U.S. size 9 (5.5 mm) straight needles
Adjust needle size as needed to obtain gauge.

NOTIONS
Waste yarn and crochet hook in size comparable to needles, for provisional cast-on
Spare needle
Tapestry needle
Needle and thread
One 1⅝" button
Separating zipper, 22–24 inches long

GAUGE
13 sts and 19 rows = 4 inches/10cm in St st with two strands of yarn held together

NOTES
Measure the front opening and buy the zipper after the sweater has been blocked and assembled. A metal zipper is authentically vintage; plastic zippers wear better and come in more colors.

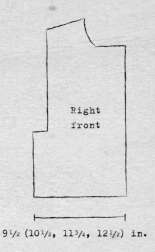

Right front

9½ (10½, 11¾, 12½) in.

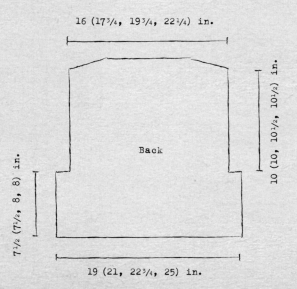

16 (17¾, 19¾, 22¼) in.

Back

10 (10, 10½, 10½) in.

7½ (7½, 8, 8) in.

19 (21, 22¾, 25) in.

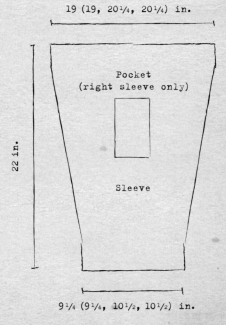

19 (19, 20¼, 20¼) in.

Pocket
(right sleeve only)

Sleeve

22 in.

9¼ (9¼, 10½, 10½) in.

BACK

With waste yarn, provisionally cast on 64 (70, 76, 84) sts. With a single strand of main yarn, work k1, p1 rib for 10 inches. Remove waste yarn from cast-on and place live stitches on the spare needle. Fold ribbing in half lengthwise. Holding the two needles together, knit each st from front needle together with corresponding st from back needle to create double-layer ribbed hem. Join in a second strand of yarn. With two strands of yarn held together, continue in St st for 2½ (2½, 3, 3) inches, beg and ending with WS rows.

Shape Armholes
Bind off 5 (5, 5, 5) sts at beg of next 2 rows—54 (60, 66, 74) sts rem.
Work even until armholes measure 10 (10, 10½, 10½) inches.

Shape Shoulders
Bind off 4 (5, 6, 7) sts at beg of next 6 rows.
Bind off rem 30 (30, 30, 32) sts.

RIGHT FRONT

With waste yarn, provisionally cast on 33 (36, 39, 43) sts. Work ribbing and make hem as for Back. Join in a second strand of yarn. With two strands of yarn held together, and slipping the first st of every RS row purlwise for a neat front edge, continue in St st for 2½ (2½, 3, 3) inches, beginning with a WS row and ending with a RS row.

Shape Armhole
Bind off 5 (5, 5, 6) sts at beg of next row— 28 (31, 34, 37) sts rem.
Work even until armhole measures 8¼ (8¼, 8¾, 8¾) inches, ending with a WS row.

Shape Neck
Bind off 11 sts at beg of next row—17 (20, 23, 26) sts rem.
Dec 1 st at neck edge of every row until 12 (15, 18, 21) sts rem.
Work 3 (3, 3, 3) rows even.

Shape Shoulder
Bind off 4 (5, 6, 7) sts at beg of every WS row 3 times.

LEFT FRONT
Work as for Right Front, reversing shaping.

SLEEVES

With waste yarn, provisionally cast on 32 (32, 36, 36) sts. With a single strand of main yarn, work k1, p1 rib for 5 inches. Make hem as for Back. Join in a second strand of yarn. With two strands of yarn held together, continue in St st beg with a WS row, inc 1 st at each end of every 4th row to 64 (64, 68, 68) sts. Work even until sleeve measures 22 inches, ending with a WS row. Bind off.

POCKET (make 1)
With two strands of yarn held together, cast on 19 sts and work in St st for 18 rows. Work 6 rows k1, p1 rib. Bind off in rib.

FINISHING
Block pieces.
Sew shoulder seams.

Collar
Beginning at right front edge with RS facing and a single strand of yarn, pick up and knit 1 st in every st and row around neckline, ending with an even number of sts. Work in k1, p1 rib for 12½ inches. Bind off loosely. Fold collar to inside and slip-stitch bound-off edge in place. Slip-stitch short edges of collar closed.

Slip-stitch pocket to right sleeve (as shown in the photograph on page 94) and attach button to center of pocket ribbing. Set sleeves into armholes. Sew side and sleeve seams. Weave in ends. Insert zipper, having bottom of coil about 1 inch from bottom of sweater and top of coil about 1 inch from top edge of collar.

OHIO KNITTING MILLS

Original Design

Winter 1967

4201 PERKINS AVENUE
CLEVELAND, O. 44103

California Dreaming

If any place provided the perfect backdrop for the 1960s, California was it. From Haight-Ashbury to Laurel Canyon—everyone who was anyone, including the likes of Joni Mitchell and Joan Didion, knew that the Golden State was where the party could be found. It was the capital of the American Dream, a playground of swooping freeways, the nexus of the counterculture, the epicenter of an era that emphasized breezy living and freewheeling, indulgent fun.

Its diverse landscape had the draw of the new Promised Land—gorgeous weather, seashores and mountaintops, movie stars and shiny cars cruising along the coastline. It was Babylon reborn—a mythical utopia fashioned by the unique sixties sensibility. This was the time of the Summer of Love, the Monterey Pop Festival, and Big Sur.

California became such an icon during this decade that it was as much a brand as a place. From orange juice to apparel, the state was a marketing scheme even more than a destination. The Midwestern knitwear industry soon realized that if it had the California tagline, it was deemed worth buying. The Ohio Knitting Mills now found itself with a long roster of California-based clients: Alice of California, Barbara Nan of California, Glover California Styling, and more.

Even companies like Campus Sportswear, though based out of Cleveland, developed an entire line of "Campus Casuals from California," looking to cash in on the West Coast allure with pieces like California Dreaming—a sweater of sunset hues and waves of different-gauged yarns—that embodied the luster of the landscape. Its boat neck and loose shape also inspire thoughts of walks on the beach or hikes through the redwood forest.

In this way, the most popular decorative motifs of the 1960s adopted an elemental language in many products, from home décor to wardrobes. The design of the times played on the merging of sun, sky, and sea, attempting to capture the luminous quality of a California sunset or the breaking waves of the Pacific Ocean.

Sweaters like California Dreaming allowed a girl to wrap herself in the West Coast dream without having to leave her home.

Knit in simple reverse Stockinette stitch, this is a great project for even beginning knitters. Seaming the sweater with the purl side out produces a richly textured surface, and the marled effect is created by holding two different shades of yarn together

---

SIZES
To fit bust 32–34 (36–38, 40–42, 44–46) inches

FINISHED MEASUREMENTS
Bust 34 (38, 42, 46) inches
Length 25¾ (26½, 27, 27¾) inches

YARN
Manos del Uruguay Wool Clásica
(100% wool; 137 yds per 100 g)
A: #72 Pumpkin, 2 (2, 3, 3) skeins
B: #14 Natural, 2 (2, 3, 3) skeins
C: #57 Raspberry, 2 (2, 3, 3) skeins

Cascade Pastaza (50% wool, 50% llama;
132 yds per 100 g)
D: #0006 Silver Gray, 2 (2, 3, 3) skeins
E: #0065 Ruby, 2 (2, 3, 3) skeins

NEEDLES
U.S. size 15 (10 mm) straight needles
Adjust needle size as needed to obtain gauge.

NOTIONS
Stitch holder
Tapestry needle

GAUGE
8 sts and 12½ rows = 4 inches/10 cm in reverse St st with two strands of yarn held together

NOTES
A range of "to fit" sizes is given because some people feel that super-bulky knits are most flattering when worn with minimal or negative ease. If you're in the negative-ease camp, you might even want to make the next size down. If you'd prefer an easy-fitting pullover to wear as a top layer, choose a size with a finished bust measurement at least 2 inches larger than your own.

STITCH INSTRUCTIONS
Stripe Pattern
19 (20, 20, 21) rows in C and E held together; 19 (20, 20, 21) rows in C and A; 19 (19, 20, 20) rows in A and D; 19 (19, 20, 20) rows in D and B

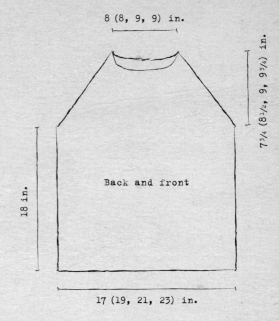

8 (8, 9, 9) in.

7¾ (8½, 9, 9¾) in.

Back and front

18 in.

17 (19, 21, 23) in.

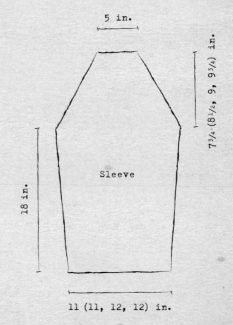

5 in.

7¾ (8½, 9, 9¾) in.

18 in.

Sleeve

11 (11, 12, 12) in.

BACK

With yarns C and E held tog, cast on 34 (38, 42, 46) sts. Knit 3 rows. Change to reverse St st, beg with a RS (purl) row, and work in Stripe patt. Work even for 53 rows. WS should be facing for next row.

Shape Raglan

Dec 1 st at each end of next row and every following 4th row 3 (2, 2, 1) times, then every WS row until 20 (20, 22, 22) sts rem.

Shape Neck

Row 1 (RS): p5, sl center 10 (10, 12, 12) sts to holder, join a second ball of yarn, and p5 to end.
Row 2 (WS): Dec 1, k to 1 st before neck edge, sl last st to stitch holder. On second side, sl first st to stitch holder, k to last 2 sts, dec 1.
Row 3 (RS): Purl.
Row 4: Rep Row 2.
   Continuing with D and B, knit 3 rows across all 16 (16, 18, 18) sts (including sts from holder). Bind off loosely.

FRONT

Work same as Back until 22 (22, 24, 24) sts rem.

Shape Neck

Row 1 (RS): p6, sl center 10 (10, 12, 12) sts to holder, join a second ball of yarn, and p6 to end.
Row 2 (WS): Dec 1, k to 1 st before neck edge, sl last st to stitch holder. On second side, sl first st to stitch holder, k to last 2 sts, dec 1.
Row 3: Purl.
Row 4: Rep Row 2.
Row 5: Purl.
Row 6: Dec 1, k to neck edge. On second side, k to last 2 sts, dec 1.
   Continuing with D and B, knit 3 rows across all 16 (16, 18, 18) sts (including sts from holder). Bind off loosely.

SLEEVES

With C and E held tog, cast on 22 (22, 24, 24) sts. Knit 3 rows. Change to reverse St st, beg with a RS (purl) row, and work in Stripe patt. Inc 1 st at each end of every 14th (10th, 10th, 8th) row to 28 (30, 32, 34) sts. Work even until you have 53 rows in reverse St st. WS should be facing for next row.

Shape Raglan

Dec 1 st at each end of next row and every following 4th row 3 times, then every WS row until 10 sts rem. Continuing with D and B, knit 3 rows. Bind off loosely.

FINISHING

Note that because of the super-bulky gauge, no selvage sts have been allowed on this pattern. We recommend seaming by butting the two edges together and overcasting (whipstitching).
   Block pieces.
   Sew raglan seams, side, and sleeve seams.
   Weave in ends.

OHIO KNITTING MILLS
Original Design

Summer   19 65

4701 PERKINS AVENUE
CLEVELAND, O. 44103

Surfer Chick

All over the radio, bands like the Beach Boys and the Surfaris were singing odes to California girls and massive wipeouts. With the tremolo of guitars providing a vibrant sound track, a cadre of surfers traveled the world in search of an endless summer. Even Annette Funicello had traded in her Mickey Mouse Club cowboy-themed costumes in favor of playing Beach Blanket Bingo with Frankie Avalon. The sand, sea, and surf represented the easy living and new openness of the 1960s.

Of course, OKM had its finger on the national style pulse, developing bright, summery knits perfect for a bonfire on the beach and loose, colorful tops like Surfer Chick.

Produced in a lightweight cotton as natural as the free-spirited girl wearing it, this knit tank was a standby for any beach bunny. Like California Dreaming, this piece also plays with elemental hues—from the ocean blue to the sunset orange. Surfer Chick also reflects the earthiness of the times without sacrificing femininity, as does the slender shape.

In this top, even girls who found themselves landlocked all summer long would practically be able to feel the ocean breeze blowing through their hair.

This fun, summery all-cotton top pairs an airy lace stitch with a more opaque Stockinette stitch with eyelets. Thread it with a belt of your favorite braid or ribbon, or wear it free and easy!

SIZES
To fit bust 30 (32, 34, 36, 38, 40, 42, 44) inches

FINISHED MEASUREMENTS
Bust 31 (32½, 35, 36½, 38, 40½, 43, 44½) inches

Length 24¼ (24½, 24¾, 25, 25¼, 25½, 25¾, 26) inches

YARN
Classic Elite Provence (100% mercerized cotton; 205 yds per 100 g)

A: Aegean Sea 2664, 1 (1, 1, 2, 2, 2, 3, 3) skeins

B: Zinnia Flower 2619, 1 (1, 1, 2, 2, 2, 3, 3) skeins

C: Slate 2628, 1 (1, 1, 2, 2, 2, 3, 3) skeins

D: Asparagus 2682, 1 (1, 1, 2, 2, 2, 3, 3) skeins

E: Natural 2616, 1 (1, 1, 2, 2, 2, 3, 3) skeins

NEEDLES
U.S. size 4 (3.5 mm) straight needles
Adjust needle size as needed to obtain gauge.

NOTIONS
Tapestry needle
Stitch holders

1½–2½ yards ribbon for waist tie (optional)
Spare knitting needle for 3-needle bind-off

GAUGE
20 sts and 30 rows = 4 inches/10 cm in Eyelet Band Pattern

STITCH INSTRUCTIONS
During armhole shaping, where there are not enough stitches to work both a yo and its corresponding dec, work the extra st(s) in St st.

Eyelet Band Pattern
Row 1 (RS): k

Row 2 (WS): p

Row 3: k15 (15, 17, 17, 17, 19, 21, 21), *k2tbl, yo; k14 (15, 16, 17, 18, 19, 20, 21); rep from * 3 times.

Row 4: p

Rows 5–6: Rep Rows 3 and 4.

Rows 7–10: Rep Rows 1 and 2.

Ridged Lace Stitch
Multiple of 2 sts + 1

Row 1 (RS): k2, *yo, k2tog tbl; rep from * to last st, k1.

Row 2 (WS): p1, *yo, p2tog; rep from * to last 2 sts, p2.

Repeat Rows 1 and 2.

Stripe Pattern
*Work Eyelet Band Pattern in C; Ridged Lace Stitch in A; Eyelet Band Pattern in E; Ridged Lace Stitch in D; Eyelet Band Pattern in B; Ridged Lace Stitch in C; Eyelet Band Pattern in D; Ridged Lace Stitch in E; Eyelet Band Pattern in A; Ridged Lace Stitch in B; rep from *.

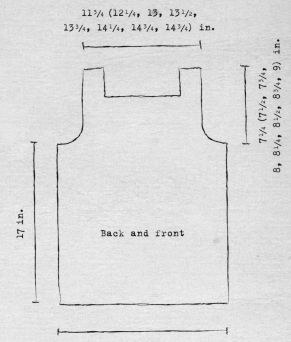

11¾ (12¼, 13, 13½, 13¾, 14¼, 14¾, 14¾) in.

7¼ (7½, 7¾, 8, 8¼, 8½, 8¾, 9) in.

17 in.

Back and front

15½ (16¼, 17½, 18¼, 19, 20¼, 21½, 22¼) in.

BACK AND FRONT (worked alike)

With C, cast on 79 (83, 89, 93, 97, 103, 109, 113) sts. Purl 1 row (WS).

Work Eyelet Band Pattern and Ridged Lace Stitch, following Stripe patt until piece measures 17 inches, ending with a WS row.

Shape Armholes

Bind off 5 (5, 5, 5, 6, 7, 9, 9) sts at beg of next 2 rows—69 (73, 79, 83, 85, 89, 91, 95) sts rem.

Bind off 1 st at beg of every row until 59 (61, 65, 67, 69, 71, 73, 73) sts rem.

Work even until armholes measure 4¼ (4½, 4¾, 5, 5¼, 5½, 5¾, 6) inches, ending with a WS row.

Shape Neck

Work 11 (11, 13, 13, 15, 15, 15, 15) sts in patt, bind off center 37 (39, 39, 41, 39, 41, 43, 43) sts, join second ball of yarn and work 11 (11, 13, 13, 15, 15, 15, 15) sts to end.

Work even on both sides at the same time until armholes measure 7¼ (7½, 7¾, 8, 8¼, 8½, 8¾, 9) inches. Place sts on holders.

FINISHING

Block pieces.

Join shoulders using 3-needle bind-off.

Sew side seams.

Weave in ends.

Weave in ribbon tie at waist level (optional).

OHIO KNITTING MILLS
Original Design

Winter   19 69

4701 PERKINS AVENUE
CLEVELAND, O. 44103

Psychedelic Scarf Set

In the fall of 1966, a former Harvard psychology pro-fessor named Timothy Leary took the stage of a New York Advertising Club press conference to deliver a message that would both shock mainstream America and become one of the most defining phrases of the sixties. "Turn on, tune in, drop out," Leary told the world.

First synthesized by a Swiss chemist in 1938, lysergic acid diethylamide—or LSD—was, at first, little more than the weird concoction of an eccentric scientist. By the 1960s, however, academics and the scientific community had realized that this seemingly harmless, odorless liquid could induce euphoric hallucinatory altered states of consciousness. This potent and mysterious drug was eventually made illegal, but not before it had left its whirling, color-drenched mark on the culture at large.

An entirely new aesthetic flourished from the hallucinatory visions of the 1960s—a world where Ken Kesey and his Merry Pranksters took an Electric Kool-Aid Acid Test, the Beatles lived in a Yellow Submarine, and lava lamps and black-light posters lit up bedrooms. Welcome to the trippy, drippy world of psychedelia.

Soon, acid-toned hues weren't just for Deadheads anymore. Marketers across America used the transcendental shapes to sell everything from cartoons to candy. The fashion world adored the bright happy colors and swirling forms of psychedelic design, like those found here in this hat-and-scarf combo.

OKM designer Elizabeth Foderaro preferred Cleveland to Haight-Ashbury, but that didn't stop her from designing otherworldly pieces like the wildly patterned sweater that inspired our Psychedelic Scarf Set. The design's chaotic colors, patterns, and shapes add a touch of Grace Slick to any winter outfit.

You can't have too many hats or scarves! Knit one piece, or the set, for a manageable first OKM project. Choose our psychedelic palette, or pick your own colors. The trippy lines are embroidered on; use our pattern or create your own.

SIZE
One size

FINISHED MEASUREMENTS
Scarf: 10¼ inches x 46½ inches
Hat circumference: 19½ inches

YARN
Classic Elite Fresco (60% wool, 30% baby alpaca, 10% angora; 164 yds per 50 g)
A: #5327 Wake Up Red, 1 skein
B: #5312 Superman Yellow, 1 skein
C: #5381 Fair Green, 2 skeins
D: #5310 Regatta, 2 skeins
E: #5301 Parchment, 4 skeins
F: #5313 Onyx, 1 skein

NEEDLES
U.S. size 1 (2.25 mm) straight needles (scarf)
Set of U.S. size 1 (2.25 mm) double-pointed needles (hat)
U.S. size 7 (4.5 mm) circular needle, 16 inches long
Adjust needle sizes as needed to obtain gauge.

NOTIONS
Tapestry needle
Embroidery needle
U.S. size E (3.5 mm) crochet hook
Stitch markers

GAUGE
28 sts and 40 rows = 4 inches/10 cm in St st

NOTES
The embroidery is done in a free-form zigzag design using a double strand of each color throughout. Refer to the photographs (opposite). Each zig moves diagonally approximately 1¼ inches horizontally and ¾ inch vertically. The zag then moves the same distance in the opposite direction. Once the first line of zigzag is stitched, follow the established pattern for the remaining lines of stitching.

Scarf

With C and straight needles, cast on 144 sts. Work in St st in the following stripe sequence: 8 rows in C; 40 rows in E; 22 rows in D; 40 rows in C; 8 rows in A; 40 rows in F; 8 rows in C; 40 rows in E; 22 rows in D; 40 rows in C; 8 rows in A; 40 rows in F; 8 rows in C; 40 rows in E; 22 rows in D; 40 rows in C; 8 rows in A; 22 rows in E; 8 rows in C.
   Bind off.

Embroidery
Note: Each wide stripe of the scarf has 3 rows of Chain st zigzag embroidery. Use a double strand of yarn throughout.

Color E Stripes (Color F Stripes)
Zigzag Row 1: Begin approximately 1 inch up from beg of stripe. Using B (B), work one row in Chain st in a zigzag motif across scarf.
Zigzag Row 2: Repeat with F (C) approximately 1 inch above the first row.
Zigzag Row 3: Repeat with F (E) approximately 1 inch above the second row.

Color C Stripes
Zigzag Row 1: Begin approximately 1 inch up from beg of stripe. Using A, work one row in Chain st in a zigzag motif across scarf.
Zigzag Row 2: Repeat with D approximately 1 inch above the first row.

Zigzag Row 3: Using D, work a third row of Chain st mirroring the second row (refer to photo).

Seam long side of scarf. Close the ends of the scarf tube with single crochet and C. Fringe ends with A.

Hat

With A and dpn, cast on 135 sts and join for working in the round. Work Garter st (knit and purl alternate rnds) for 8 rnds. Change to C and work 46 rnds in St st.

Crown Decreases
Change to D and dpns.
Rnd 1: *k45, pm; rep from * to end.
Rnd 2: *Knit to 3 sts before marker, ssk, k2, ssk; rep from * twice more—129 sts rem.
   Rep Rnd 2 until 15 sts rem. Break yarn, thread through rem sts, pull tight, and fasten off. Weave in ends.

Embroidery
Note: Use a double strand of yarn throughout.
Zigzag Row 1: Begin approximately ½ inch above the Garter st hatband. Using F, work one row of zigzag motif in Chain st around hat.
Zigzag Row 2: Repeat with E approximately ½ inch above first line of embroidery, following the established zigzag pattern.
Zigzag Row 3: Using E, work a third row of

Chain st mirroring the second row (refer to photos).
Zigzag Row 4: Using B, work a fourth row of Chain st approximately ½ inch above the last row, following the established zigzag pattern.

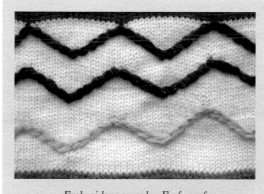
Embroidery on color E of scarf

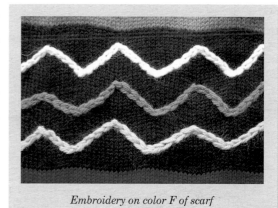
Embroidery on color F of scarf

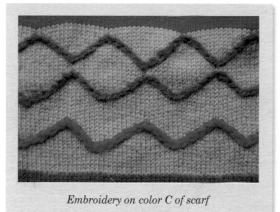
Embroidery on color C of scarf

OHIO KNITTING MILLS

Original Design

Fall ___ 19 62

4701 PERKINS AVENUE
CLEVELAND, O. 44103

The Mod

Just like their American counterparts, British teens of the 1960s were rejecting Mum and Dad's old mores in favor of a new and energetic expression. Calling themselves "mods," these English teens had a distinct fascination with authentic American blues and soul music as well as a taste for the finer things in life—tailor-made Italian suits, streamlined scooters, French New Wave cinema, existentialist philosophy, and weekend-long parties. Whether dancing the night away to soul 45s or racing Vespas around London, to be a mod was to be cool, sharp, hip, and smart.

While the term was first coined in the late 1950s and strictly referred to the attitude of modern jazz and its fans, its meaning soon expanded to include an entire society of forward-looking cultural pioneers, giving rise to such bands as the Kinks, the Yardbirds, and the Creation. By the early 1960s, the mod movement was as much a lifestyle as it was a musical preference. Mods refused the class-obsessed rigidity of their parents. They fancied themselves worldly figures unanchored by social expectations; too good for manual labor, too free for monogamy, and too cool for school.

The mod movement was also looking toward New York's art scene for inspiration. From the Campbell's soup cans of Andy Warhol to the pixilated comic book paintings of Roy Lichtenstein, the pop art movement appropriated banal objects from consumer culture and re-rendered them with stylized, ironic techniques. This work emphasized a chic detachment and criticism of mainstream culture that particularly resonated with the mods, who resisted what they viewed as inauthentic and outdated forms of mainstream culture. British mods eventually folded this pop art aesthetic into their own look: bold colors and oversized patterns, such as in The Mod sweater, became a preferred look.

The popular media quickly seized on the novelty and spirit of this "happening scene," and it wasn't long before a new brand of cool began influencing mainstream culture. As soon as British bands like the Beatles and the Who invaded the States, both the mod attitude and pop art aesthetic were being infused into the establishment's idea of stylishness.

With a nod to the swingers in London as well as to the pop artists in New York, The Mod has all the right elements of tailored cool: a turtleneck and an oversized diamond motif in striking colors. The piece also reflects a certain camp style of the new high art, as well as the carefree attitude of scooter-riding teens.

Even though the front pattern is bold and complex, it's actually rather easy to knit once you get into the rhythm.

SIZES
Men's S (M, L, XL)

FINISHED MEASUREMENTS
Chest 37 (40, 43½, 47) inches
Length 26 (26¾, 27¼, 28¼) inches

YARN
Cascade Yarns Greenland (100% superwash wool; 137 yds per 100 g)
MC: #3528 Ginger, 8 (8, 9, 10) skeins
CC1: #3527 Sunflower, 2 (3, 3, 3) skeins
CC2: #3529 Chocolate, 2 (2, 2, 3) skeins

NEEDLES
U.S. size 8 (5 mm) straight needles
U.S. size 7 (4.5 mm) straight needles
U.S. size 7 (4.5 mm) circular needle,
16 inches long
Adjust needle sizes as needed to obtain gauge.

NOTIONS
Row counter
Tapestry needle

GAUGE
17½ sts and 25 rows = 4 inches/10 cm in St st on larger needles

NOTES
Diamonds on the sweater front are worked in intarsia following the chart on page 114. When knitting is complete, the horizontal and vertical lines are embroidered in chain stitch.

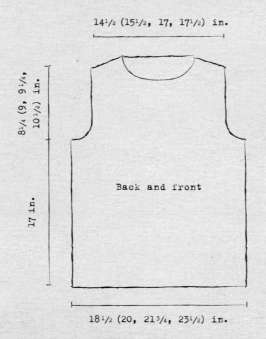

14½ (15½, 17, 17½) in.

8¼ (9, 9¼, 10½) in.

17 in.

Back and front

18½ (20, 21¾, 23½) in.

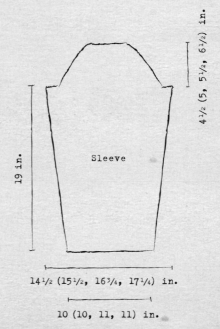

4½ (5, 5½, 6½) in.

19 in.

Sleeve

14½ (15½, 16¾, 17¼) in.

10 (10, 11, 11) in.

BACK

With MC and smaller straight needles, cast on 82 (88, 96, 104) sts. Work in k1, p1 rib for 2½ inches (15 rows), inc 1 st on last row—83 (89, 97, 105) sts total. Change to larger needles and work in St st for 90 rows, ending with a WS row.

Shape Armholes

Bind off 5 sts at beg of next 2 rows.

Dec 1 st at each end of next row and on every following RS row to 65 (69, 75, 79) sts.

Work even until you have a total of 144 (148, 152, 160) rows from ribbing.

Shape Shoulders

Bind off 5 (6, 6, 7) sts at beg of next 4 rows.

Bind off 6 (6, 7, 7) sts at beg of next 2 rows.

Bind off rem 33 (33, 37, 37) sts.

FRONT

With MC and smaller needles, cast on 82 (88, 96, 104) sts. Work in k1, p1 rib for 2½ inches (15 rows), inc 1 st on last row— 83 (89, 97, 105) sts total. Change to larger needles and work following chart (page 114). Row 1 is a RS row.

SLEEVES

With MC and smaller straight needles, cast on 46 (46, 50, 50) sts. Work in k1, p1 rib for 2½ inches, inc 1 st on last row —47 (47, 51, 51) sts. Change to larger needles and work

in St st for 7 (5, 7, 5) rows, ending with RS facing for next row.

Inc row: k2, m1, k to last 2 sts, m1, k2— 49 (49, 53, 53) sts total.

Rep Inc row on every following 8th (6th, 8th, 6th) row to 65 (69, 75, 77) sts.

Work even until sleeve measures 19 inches.

Shape Cap

Bind off 5 sts at beg of next 2 rows —55 (59, 65, 67) sts rem.

Dec 1 st at each end of next row and on every following RS row until 29 sts rem.

Bind off 3 sts at beg of next 4 rows.

Bind off rem 17 sts.

FINISHING

Block pieces.

Seam shoulders.

Collar

With circular needle and MC, RS facing, beg at shoulder, pick up and knit 3 sts for every 4 rows and 1 st in every bound-off st around neck, ending with an even number of stitches. Work k1, p1 rib in the round for 5½ inches. Bind off loosely in rib.

Set sleeves into armholes. Sew side and sleeve seams. Weave in ends.

Embroidery

Note: Refer to the chart and the photograph.

Vertical Lines

At center front, beg just above the rib, work Chain st beg bet middle of CC motif using a single strand of MC. Work one Chain st per row of knitting. Continue up center front to the neckline.

At each small diamond on either side of chest, work Chain st in the middle of each motif using MC. Repeat for bottom half-diamonds beg just above rib.

Horizontal Lines

Determine center row of the widest part of the large lower diamond. Beginning at left side seam with MC, work one row of Chain st following the same knit row across the width of the sweater. Repeat two more times at the second large upper diamond and on either side of the shoulders.

Embroidery Guide

SWEATERS ON THE SILVER SCREEN

The third in a line of Midwestern knitting-mill men, Pete Woodworth was the kind of modest Minnesotan who never expected to go Hollywood. His grandfather Walker Woodworth founded the Stone Knitting Mills along with Harry Stone. Pete was keeping his family's legacy afloat at the Winona Knitting Mills, the southeastern Minnesota mill opened by Stone and taken over by the Woodworth family in the mid-1940s. Winona continued to produce men's sweaters for Ohio Knitting Mills and grew to be one of the largest manufacturers of knitwear in the country. As OKM shifted its focus to women's wear, Winona continued to produce iconic men's sweaters.

One day in 1998, Pete was watching a trailer for a new movie from Joel and Ethan Coen called *The Big Lebowski*. As Jeff Bridges shuffled around the screen as "The Dude," his choice of cardigan quickly caught Pete's attention. The vintage Chief Joseph pattern and shawl collar were unmistakable: The Dude was sporting a Winona Knitting Mills original. "I knew right away," Pete recalls. "We made it for over ten years, for Pendleton. It was 100 percent wool and weighed almost four pounds. In fact, it was the heaviest sweater we ever made and one of the most expensive at the time."

Through a friend who had been working on the film

You make each day a special day by just your being you.

Mister Rogers's mother, Nancy, always handknit the sweaters he wore on TV. After her death in 1981, Fred Rogers started wearing sweaters made by various companies, including OKM sweaters like this one.

with the Coen brothers, Pete got in contact with Bridges, who had come across the Winona Mills sweater in a prop shop in Hollywood. As the star later wrote Pete, as soon as he spotted the cardigan, he knew it was perfect for The Dude. Pete and his wife were invited to the premiere of the film, where Pete's wife sported a woman's version of the sweater, to the delight of the paparazzi.

The Big Lebowski wasn't Winona's first foray into popular culture. During the early 1980s, Pete's young son was a huge fan of *Mister Rogers' Neighborhood*. And Fred Rogers appeared to be a big fan of cardigans. Pete's wife suggested that they send Mister Rogers a few Winona Mills samples, just as a kind gesture.

The studio got right back to Pete, asking that he send more of Winona's designs. For the next five years, every several months Pete sent Mister Rogers a batch of sweaters, some of which appeared on air. Mister Rogers even featured the Winona Knitting Mills on a field-trip segment of the show.

To this day, Winona's brushes with fame still make Pete beam with pride. "To have our sweaters be part of something so incredible is just remarkable for me," he says.

OHIO KNITTING MILLS

Original Design

Fall   19<u>65</u>

4701 PERKINS AVENUE
CLEVELAND, O. 44103

Mondrian Skyline

Just as the Abstract Expressionist looked to the art scene for its inspiration, Mondrian Skyline also mimicked modern art. While sharply tailored suits became the uniform of mod men, the shift dress became a preferred silhouette of the 1960s "it girls," from Jane Fonda to Grace Slick.

Haute couture designers like Halston as well as Heartland apparel manufacturers like OKM were all producing these fashionable and form-fitting pieces—the pinnacle of mid-sixties sleek style. Not only did the shift offer a modern and sexy silhouette, but it also provided a shapely blank canvas for a wide range of colorful and dynamic graphic patterns.

By the late 1960s a more urbane and minimalist aesthetic was emerging, one influenced by Scandinavian design's simple and sleek lines, as well as the cool elegance of the jet set. Uncluttered graphics and clean sculptural forms were this look's hallmark. And it was Yves Saint Laurent who, in the fall of 1965, took the fashion world by storm when he debuted his "Mondrian" day dresses on the Paris runway. Influenced by the *Composition* series of Piet Mondrian, the grandfather of modernism and the most iconic artist of the Dutch De Stijl movement, Saint Laurent literally translated his idol's geometric paintings into dresses, making them wearable works of art.

It's obvious that this fashion breakthrough caught the attention of OKM. The Mondrian Skyline is an almost literal translation of the high-end YSL piece. But while Saint Laurent's dresses were bought by society luminaries for thousands of dollars, Elizabeth Foderaro's architectural design was sold in department stores across the country, and could be purchased for less than $30, making the ultimate in elegance accessible to Main Street America.

This project uses basic techniques most knitters can handle; the graphic color blocks are created by seaming together striped panels. Although the amount of knitting involved might be a bit time-consuming, the results are *très moderne!*

SIZES
To fit bust 32 (34, 36, 38, 40, 42) inches

FINISHED MEASUREMENTS
Bust 32 (34, 36, 38, 40, 42) inches
Length 38 inches

YARN
Classic Elite Classic One Fifty (100% wool; 150 yds per 50 g)
MC: #7202 Daisy, 7 (7, 8, 8, 9, 9) skeins
CC1: #7213 Black, 2 (2, 2, 3, 3, 3) skeins
CC2: #7258 Radish, 1 (1, 1, 2, 2, 2) skeins

NEEDLES
U.S. size 6 (4 mm) straight needles
U.S. size 4 (3.5 mm) straight needles
Adjust needle sizes as needed to obtain gauge.

NOTIONS
Stitch markers
Tapestry needle
Crochet hook (optional)
One ⅜-inch black button
Needle and thread

GAUGE
24 sts and 32 rows = 4 inches/10 cm in St st on larger needles

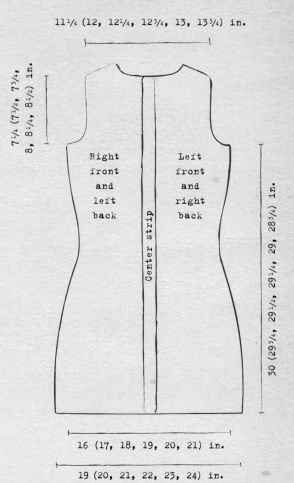

11¼ (12, 12¼, 12¾, 13, 13¾) in.

7¼ (7½, 7¾, 8, 8¼, 8½) in.

Right front and left back

Center strip

Left front and right back

30 (29¾, 29½, 29¼, 29, 28¾) in.

16 (17, 18, 19, 20, 21) in.

19 (20, 21, 22, 23, 24) in.

RIGHT BACK

With smaller needles and MC, cast on 61 (64, 67, 70, 73, 76) sts. Work 12 rows in St st, beg with a knit row and ending with a purl row. Change to larger needles. Place a marker at end of last row. Work even in St st until piece measures 4¼ inches from marker.

Work bottom stripes as follows: *8 rows CC1, 10 rows MC; rep from * twice more, then work 8 rows CC1. After 5th CC1 stripe, continue in MC only until top stripes begin.

AT THE SAME TIME, when piece measures 6 inches from marker, shape waist as follows:

Dec row (RS): k1, ssk, k to end—60 (63, 66, 69, 72, 75) sts rem.

Rep Dec row on every following 6th row 10 times, then every following 4th row until 40 (43, 46, 49, 52, 55) sts rem.

After waist decreases are complete, work 4 inches even, ending with a WS row.

Inc row (RS): k2, m1, k to end—41 (44, 47, 50, 53, 56) sts total.

Rep Inc row on every following 8th row to 46 (49, 52, 55, 58, 61) sts.

AT THE SAME TIME, when work measures 23 inches from marker, work top stripes as follows: 8 rows in CC1; 10 rows in MC; 8 rows in CC1; 10 rows in MC; 8 rows in CC1; 26 rows in CC2; 8 rows in CC1; then work to end of piece in MC.

AT THE SAME TIME, when work measures 30 (29¾, 29½, 29¼, 29, 28¾) inches from marker, ending with a WS row, shape armhole as follows: Bind off 6 sts at beg of next row—40 (43, 46, 49, 52, 55) sts rem.

Work 1 row even.

Bind off 0 (0, 0, 2, 3, 4) sts at beg of next row. Work 1 row even. (If number is 0, omit these 2 rows)—40 (43, 46, 47, 49, 51) sts rem.

Dec row (RS): ssk, k to end—39 (42, 45, 46, 48, 50) sts rem.

Rep Dec row on every following RS row until 32 (34, 35, 36, 37, 39) sts rem.

Work even until armhole measures 7¼ (7½, 7¾, 8, 8¼, 8½) inches, ending with a WS row.

Shape Neck and Shoulders

Bind off 6 sts at beg of next row, k to end.

Next row (WS): Bind off 15 (17, 17, 17, 17, 19) sts, p to end.

Next row: Bind off 6 sts, k to end.

Next row: Purl.

Bind off rem 5 (5, 6, 7, 8, 8) sts.

LEFT BACK

Work as for Right Back, reversing shaping and placing stripes as follows:

When work measures 22 inches from marker, work top stripes as follows: 8 rows in CC1; 8 rows in CC2; 8 rows in CC1; 28 rows in MC; 8 rows in CC1; 10 rows in MC; 8 rows in CC1; 10 rows in CC2; 8 rows in CC1; then work to end of piece in MC.

LEFT FRONT

With smaller needles and MC, cast on 61 (64, 67, 70, 73, 76) sts. Work 12 rows in St st, beg with a knit row and ending with a purl row. Change to larger needles. Place a marker at end of last row. Continue to work even in St st until piece measures 6 inches from marker, ending with a WS row.

Shape Waist

Dec row (RS): k1, ssk, k to end—60 (63, 66, 69, 72, 75) sts rem.

Rep Dec row on every following 6th row 10 times, then every following 4th row—40 (43, 46, 49, 52, 55) sts rem.

AT THE SAME TIME, when work measures 8 inches from marker, work bottom stripes as follows: 8 rows in CC1; 10 rows in MC; 8 rows in CC1; 10 rows in MC; 8 rows in CC1. After third CC1 stripe, continue in MC only until top stripes begin.

After waist decreases are complete, work 4 inches even, ending with a WS row.

Inc row (RS): k2, m1, k to end—41 (42, 47, 50, 53, 56) sts.

Rep Inc row on every following 8th row to 46 (49, 52, 55, 58, 61) sts.

AT THE SAME TIME, when work measures 25½ inches from marker, work top stripes as follows: 8 rows in CC1; 26 rows in CC2; 8 rows in CC1. After second CC1 stripe, continue in MC only.

AT THE SAME TIME, when work measures 30 (29¾, 29½, 29¼, 29, 28¾) inches from marker, ending with a WS row, shape armhole as follows: Bind off 6 sts at beg of next row—40 (43, 46, 49, 52, 55) sts rem.

Work 1 row even.

Bind off 0 (0, 0, 2, 3, 4) sts at beg of next row. Work 1 row even. (If number is 0, omit these 2 rows)—40 (43, 46, 47, 49, 51) sts rem.

Dec row (RS): ssk, k to end—39 (42, 45, 46, 48, 50) sts rem.

Rep Dec row on every following RS row until 32 (34, 35, 36, 37, 39) sts rem.

Work even until armhole measures 5½ (5¾, 6, 6¼, 6½, 6¾) inches, ending with a RS row.

Shape Neck

Bind off 9 (10, 10, 10, 10, 11) sts at beg of next row.

Work 1 row even.

Bind off 3 sts at beg of next row.

Dec row (RS): Knit to last 2 sts, k2tog.

Rep Dec row on every following RS row until 17 (17, 18, 19, 20, 20) sts rem.

Work even until armhole measures 7¼ (7½, 7¾, 8, 8¼, 8½) inches, ending with a WS row.

Shape Shoulder

Bind off 6 sts at beg of next two RS rows.

Work 1 row even.

Bind off rem 5 (5, 6, 7, 8, 8) sts.

RIGHT FRONT

Work same as Left Front, reversing shaping and placing stripes as follows:

When work measures 11¾ inches from marker, work bottom stripes as follows: 8 rows in CC1; 26 rows in CC2; 8 rows in CC1. After second CC1 stripe, continue in MC only until top stripes begin.

When piece measures 30 (29¾, 29½, 29¼, 29, 28¾) inches from marker (at the same time you begin armhole shaping), work top stripes as follows: 8 rows in CC1; 10 rows in MC; 8 rows in CC1. After 2nd CC1, continue in MC only to end of piece.

CENTER FRONT STRIP

With smaller needles and black, cast on 10 sts. Work 12 rows in St st. Change to larger needles and place a marker at end of last row. Work even in St st until strip measures 35¾ inches from marker. Bind off.

CENTER BACK STRIP

With smaller needles and black, cast on 10 sts. Work 12 rows in St st. Change to larger needles and place a marker at end of last row. Continue to work even in St st until strip measures 35 inches from marker, ending with a WS row.

Next row: k5, turn.

Work on these 5 sts until strip measures 37¼ inches from marker. Bind off.

Join yarn to rem 5 sts and work until strip measures 37¼ inches from marker. Bind off.

FINISHING

Back Neck Slit

With CC1 and smaller needles, RS facing, beg at neck edge, pick up and knit 2 sts for every 3 rows down right side of neck slit in center back strip, and up left side. Turn. Bind off knitwise.

Use mattress stitch and MC to seam Center Front Strip between Left and Right Fronts. Repeat for Center Back Strip and Left and Right Backs.

Block pieces.

Neckband

Seam Front to Back at shoulders. With smaller needles and CC1, beg at left side of back slit with RS facing, pick up and knit 1 st in every bound-off st and 3 sts for every 4 rows around neck edge, making sure to have an even number of sts. Work k1, p1 rib for 1 inch. Bind off in rib.

Make small button loop on right side of back neckband with CC1 and crochet chain (or use sewn button loop). Sew button opposite.

Armhole Edgings

With smaller needles and CC1, beg at underarm with RS facing, pick up and knit 1 st in every bound-off st and 3 sts for every 4 rows around armhole edge, making sure to have an even number of sts. Work k1, p1 rib for 1 inch. Bind off in rib.

Sew side seams.

Turn up hem and slip-stitch in place, taking care not to let sts show through on RS.

1980s WOMEN'S SWEATERS

Too much is just about right

OEM's creativity and palettes peaked in the sixties, coinciding with a shift of all its production over to women's wear. Mirroring the exploding cultural influences and social freedoms of the era, these sweaters gave mass-market America fun tops in original patterns and vibrant colors, each ready to complement stirrup pants, jeans, or capri pants. The styles and shapes referenced looks coming from the counterculture, which was an endless source of voyeuristic fascination for the mainstream.

PROJECTS IN THIS CHAPTER

The 1970s

THREADS OF MANY COLORS

America has always been a place of assimilation. As different waves of ethnic groups arrived here, they strived to replace the customs of the "old country" with the American way. In order to fit in, newcomers anglicized their names, banished their native tongues in favor of English, and did whatever else was necessary in order to wash away any trace of difference with the hope of becoming part of the mainstream.

However, by the 1970s, American society was well on its way to replacing conformity with individuality. The seventies signaled a time when people were finally encouraged to embrace their heritage and accentuate their differences. From children's television shows that encouraged uniqueness, like *Sesame Street,* to sociopolitical movements like the Black Panthers and the inception of bilingual education in California's schools, Americans were embracing a myriad of cultural tropes. To cite just one example, housewives co-opted a more natural, indigenous-inspired look, with such touches as Native American prints and flowing, untamed manes. Quaintness was out and exoticism was in.

At the same time, the women's liberation movement was gaining momentum. Women were moving beyond their basic roles as domestic caretakers. Their duties and interests became more dynamic and manifold, extending beyond the home and their immediate neighborhoods. Women were going to college in record numbers, making inroads into corporate boardrooms, and, inspired by the examples set by Barbara Jordan, Golda Meir, and other leaders, entering politics to effect social change. And both men and women were incorporating Eastern religious practices and social justice issues into their lives.

Meanwhile, the American garment industry was struggling to remain profitable as a flood of cheap imported goods made the domestic market more competitive. Where Cleveland was home to more than twenty-five knitting mills during the first half of the century, by the mid-1970s, it had fewer than ten remaining in operation. Still, Leonard Rand managed to thrive in a world where American garment manufacturing was becoming a thing of the past.

The Ohio Knitting Mills continued to churn out up-to-the-minute pieces that remained in high demand. The company's poncho, especially, became a major best seller, as OKM designed ethnic-influenced garb for the new, worldly woman, and entire lines of separates for the plethora of fashions aimed at teens—a demographic that, by the 1970s, was firmly established in mainstream culture and the marketplace.

OHIO KNITTING MILLS
Original Design

Fall   19 72

4701 PERKINS AVENUE
CLEVELAND, O. 44103

The Outsider

Since the inception of the company, the Ohio Knitting Mills was always staffed with a wide variety of ethnicities. Cleveland has long been a magnet for immigrants, whether Germans and Italians fleeing fascism in the 1930s, Czechs and Hungarians escaping Soviet repression in the 1950s and '60s, or the Cuban refugees of the 1960s. And they were always sure to find a home at OKM.

Because many established Americans wouldn't do such tedious work for low textile-mill wages, immigrants often found ample opportunities amid the warp, circular, and Jacquard machines and sewing floors of the knitting mills. Many of these immigrants also brought the added benefit of needle-trade backgrounds from the old country, and once here, they worked hard to share in the American Dream and become assimilated in their new environment.

The factory floor wasn't the only place where the influx of ethnic groups left its mark. Along with dreams for a better life, many of these groups also brought along their rich ancestral traditions and cultures, which often helped spark the imaginations of Ohio Knitting Mills designers.

Elizabeth Foderaro, herself the daughter of Sicilian immigrants, began infusing ethnic influences into her already dynamic designs, such as the elaborate patterns of Eastern European folk costumes and the nontraditional shapes of Latin America. This blending of international flavors perfectly fit the technical versatility of the Ohio Knitting Mills' distinct warp knitting techniques. As a result, the company created pieces, like The Outsider, that easily could have come from a bazaar in Marrakech or a Navajo trading post in Arizona.

From the sweater's diamond pattern down to its tunic shape and wide sleeves, this sweater would have made any girl feel like a worldly jet-setter, ready to fly off on an adventure in Brazil or a trek through the Himalayas.

Alternating stripes of Stockinette and Seed stitch in a thick-and-thin yarn provide a rich background for the lozenge-shaped Satin-stitch embroidery.

SIZES
To fit bust 30 (34, 38, 42, 46) inches

FINISHED MEASUREMENTS
Bust 32 (36, 40, 44, 48) inches
Length 23¾ (23¾, 24¼, 24¼, 25) inches

YARN
Noro Cash Iroha (40% silk, 30% lambswool, 20% cashmere, 10% nylon; 99 yds per 40 g)
A: #01 Natural White, 4 (5, 6, 6, 7) skeins
B: #101 Lime Green, 4 (5, 6, 6, 7) skeins
C: #103 Lavender, 3 (4, 4, 5, 5) skeins

NEEDLES
U.S. size 8 (5 mm) straight needles
U.S. size 7 (4.5 mm) circular needle, 16 inches long
Adjust needle sizes as needed to obtain gauge.

NOTIONS
Stitch markers
Stitch holders
Tapestry needle
U.S. size H (5 mm) crochet hook
Two U.S. size 7 (4.5 mm) double-pointed needles (optional)

GAUGE
18 sts and 28 rows = 4 inches/10 cm in St st on larger needles

---

NOTES
Worked in stripes of color, alternating Stockinette and Seed stitch. The lozenge shapes are embroidered in an approximation of satin stitch, using a double strand of yarn.

STITCH INSTRUCTIONS
Seed Stitch
Multiple of 2 sts
Row 1: *k1, p1; rep from * to end.
Row 2: *p1, k1; rep from * to end.
Rep Rows 1 and 2.
Multiple of 2 sts + 1
Row 1: *k1, p1; rep from * to last st, k1.
Rep Row 1.

Stripe Pattern
Work 3½ inches in St st with B, ending with a WS row.
Knit 1 RS row with C.
Work 1½ inches in Seed st with C, ending with a RS row.
Purl 1 WS row with C.

Work 3½ inches in St st with A, ending with a WS row.
Knit 1 RS row with B.
Work 1½ inches in Seed st with B, ending with a RS row.
Purl 1 WS row with B.
Work 3½ inches in St st with C, ending with a WS row.
Knit 1 RS row with A.
Work 1½ inches in Seed st with A, ending with a RS row.
Purl 1 WS row with A.
Work 3½ inches in St st with B, ending with a WS row.
Knit 1 RS row with C.
Work 1½ inches in Seed st with C, ending with a RS row.
Purl 1 WS row with C.
Work to end of piece in St st with A.

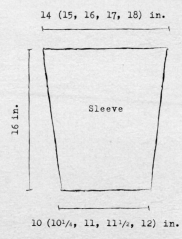

10½ (10¾, 11, 11¼, 11½) in.

23 (23, 23½, 23½, 24) in.

Back and front

16 (18, 20, 22, 24) in.

14 (15, 16, 17, 18) in.

16 in.

Sleeve

10 (10¼, 11, 11½, 12) in.

BACK

With B and larger needles, cast on 74 (83, 92, 101, 110) sts. Work in Stripe patt until piece measures 16 (15½, 16, 15½, 15) inches. Place a marker at each end of last row to indicate base of armholes. Work even until piece measures 23 (23, 23½, 23½, 24) inches, ending with a WS row.

Shape Shoulders

Bind off 5 (6, 7, 9, 10) sts at beg of next 2 rows.
Bind off 4 (6, 7, 8, 10) sts at beg of next 2 rows.
Bind off 4 (5, 7, 8, 9) sts at beg of next 2 rows.
Place rem 48 (49, 50, 51, 52) sts on holder.

FRONT

Work same as Back until piece measures 21½ (21½, 22, 22, 22½) inches, ending with a WS row.

Shape Neck and Shoulders

Next row (RS): k28 (32, 36, 40, 44), place center 18 (19, 20, 21, 22) sts on a holder, join a second ball of yarn and k28 (32, 36, 40, 44).

Working both sides at the same time with separate balls of yarn in St st, bind off 4 sts at each neck edge 2 times, then 3 sts at each neck edge once, then 2 sts at each neck edge once, then dec 1 st at each neck edge on every second row twice.

AT THE SAME TIME, when Front measures 23

(23, 23½, 23½, 24) inches, shape shoulders as for Back.

SLEEVES

With B and larger needles, cast on 46 (48, 52, 53, 56) sts. Work in Stripe patt, inc 1 st at each end of every 8th (8th, 8th, 6th, 6th) row to 66 (70, 74, 79, 83) sts. Work even until sleeve measures approximately 16 inches, ending with a completed Seed st stripe in A. Bind off.

FINISHING

Block pieces.
Sew shoulder seams.

Embroidery

All embroidery is done with a double strand of yarn. Satin st is worked in a lozenge shape over the Seed st stripes.

Body

Begin with the top Seed st stripe (in C). Using a double strand of B, work 5 lozenge shapes in Satin st across the middle of the stripe. Lozenges should be approximately 2½ inches long and ¾ inch high and equally spaced across the work.

For the second Seed st stripe (in A), repeat above embroidery using C.

For the third Seed st stripe (in B), repeat above embroidery using A.

For the bottom Seed st stripe (in C), work 7 lozenge shapes across the middle of the Seed st stripe using a double strand of B. Each should be approximately 1½ inches long and ¾ inch high, equally spaced across the work.

Sleeves

Beginning with the top Seed st stripe (in A), work 6 lozenge shapes in C, as on the body. Each should be approximately 1¾ inches long and ¾ inch high, equally spaced across the work.

For the middle Seed st stripe (in B), repeat the top sleeve embroidery using A.

For the bottom Seed st stripe (in C), work 5 lozenge shapes using B.

Weave in ends. Block lightly to even out stitching.

Collar

With circular needle and A, RS facing and beg at left shoulder, pick up and knit 52 (53, 54, 55, 56) sts across front neck including sts on holder, then knit 48 (49, 50, 51, 52) sts from back neck stitch holder. Work k1, p1 rib in the round for 2½ inches. Bind off loosely in rib.

Attach sleeves to body. Sew side and sleeve seams. Weave in ends. Work 1 round of single crochet with B around bottom edge of body and sleeves.

For optional waist tie, cast on 4 sts with dpn and A and work I-cord to desired length.

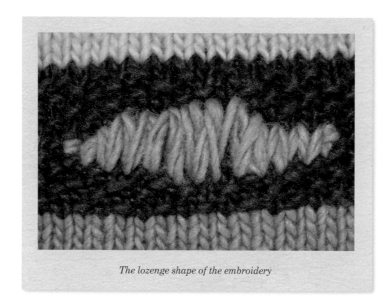

The lozenge shape of the embroidery

ELIZABETH FODERARO

When Leonard Rand took over his father-in-law's company in 1947, there was no question that he'd keep Elizabeth Foderaro on as the Ohio Knitting Mills head designer.

Elizabeth had started working at Stone Knitting Mills as a teenager, apprenticing under the company's former head designer, Sophie Zipken. The daughter of Italian immigrants, Elizabeth showed an aptitude for the detail-oriented work of knitwear design. After graduating from high school, she went to work full-time while attending design school at night. By the late 1940s she'd already designed dozens of lines for the company. Her ski sweaters, such as the Lonesome Pine and the Golden Goose, had become best sellers.

Under her design leadership at Ohio Knitting Mills, Elizabeth expanded the company's production to include a variety of women's separates, from pieces like Le Petit Pull et Amie to her many colorful cardigans. She'd create more than a hundred looks each fall, and up to forty pieces

Elizabeth Foderaro in the early 1990s.

each spring. Her designs were then sold to major retailers like Sears and Nordstrom, as well as fashion labels like Bobbie Brooks and Lane Bryant.

In a 1952 profile in the Cleveland *Plain Dealer*, Elizabeth remarked, "The sweater is now a basic part of the fashion wardrobe. Style, color, even intricate designs knit into the fabric make sweaters what they are today."

Elizabeth often looked toward the fashion coming out of Europe to inspire her own work—like the Mondrian Skyline, which is directly influenced by the modernist shifts of Yves Saint Laurent's fall 1965 line. "One thing gives you an idea for something else," she said. "An Italian style, for instance, might offer inspiration for styles here."

In the 1970s, Leonard promoted Elizabeth to vice president of the company. Until her death in 1996, it was her creative interpretations of the changing trends that kept Ohio Knitting Mills clothing so fresh and relevant.

The Grooviest Poncho

Nothing exudes 1970s boho breeziness more than the knit poncho. Its origins lie in the indigenous cultures of Central and South America, where the patterned bright bands of color and elaborate graphics were traditionally layered with meaning to express social status as well as familial history. The exploding counterculture scene during the Vietnam War era was particularly interested in the world south of the border—an exotic yet inexpensive destination where draft dodgers could hide out and pseudo-spiritualists, inspired by Carlos Castaneda's tales, could absorb shamanistic "teachings." And though ponchos appeared in American fashion well before the 1970s, only then did this versatile piece become a mainstay of hippies and homemakers alike, thanks to its ease of wear and ethnic allusions. During the late sixties and early seventies, the poncho had become a familiar accoutrement of rock stars and folkies like Carole King and Neil Young.

The huge demand for these garments also saved the Ohio Knitting Mills from financial disaster. With the onslaught of foreign manufacturing seriously threatening the American textile industry, OKM was facing potential ruin. But just as the company was struggling to stay afloat (as were the rest of Cleveland's garment businesses), Elizabeth Foderaro came to the rescue with her most iconic design yet: The Grooviest Poncho. As she had for decades, Foderaro looked to popular trends in order to keep the company's fashion lines current. She designed numerous poncho styles full of color and fringe that would easily appeal to the playful sensibility of everyday America. Sold at affordable prices, this poncho quickly became the company's number-one seller. The staff worked overtime to meet the demand for them, and business revived even as many of OKM's local competitors withered away.

In fact, OKM ponchos became so prolific that Frank Zappa touched on their ubiquity in his 1973 song "Camarillo Brillo," singing: "Is that a real poncho, or a Sears poncho?" If it was bought at Sears, it was almost certainly an Ohio Knitting Mills design.

It's easy to sympathize with Zappa's dismay with the mallification of the counterculture. But had he known that it was the "inauthentic" poncho that kept the few remnants of the American textile industry alive, we suspect he'd have given the company a pass.

This project is knit in five separate sections and then seamed together for easier handling. And yes, fringed!

- -

SIZE
One size

FINISHED MEASUREMENTS
Bottom circumference: 77 inches
Length (not including collar or fringe): 24 inches

YARN
Manos del Uruguay Wool Clásica (100% wool; 137 yds per 100 g)
MC: #S Magenta, 7 skeins
CC1: #14 Natural, 2 skeins
CC2: #08 Black, 1 skein

NEEDLES
U.S. size 8 (5 mm) straight or circular needles
Adjust needle size as needed to obtain gauge.

NOTIONS
Tapestry needle
Five buttons
Needle and thread to match MC
Five size 8 or size 10 sew-on snaps
U.S. size H (5 mm) crochet hook

GAUGE
15 sts and 22 rows = 4 inches/10 cm in St st

NOTES
Poncho is worked in five panels from the bottom edge to the neck. Given the width of the panels at cast-on, you may find it easier to work back and forth on a circular needle.
Border on chart shows pattern repeat. Pattern is worked in stranded colorwork. Carry the yarn not in use loosely along the back of the work.

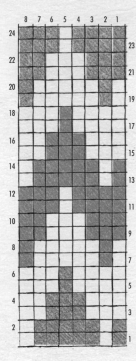

Chevron

BACK

With MC, cast on 78 sts. Work 7 rows in St st, ending with a WS row. Dec 1 st at each end of next row and on following 8th row—74 sts rem. Work 1 WS row even.

Work Rows 1–24 of Chevron chart (opposite), beg with St 1 and ending with St 8.

Dec 1 st at each end of next row, then every following 8th row until 62 sts rem. Work 1 WS row even.

Work Rows 1–24 of chart, beg with St 1 and ending with St 8.

Dec 1 st at each end of next row, then every 2nd row until 38 sts rem.

Bind off.

RIGHT FRONT

With MC, cast on 37 sts.

Row 1 (WS): Purl to last 4 sts, (k1, p1) twice.

Row 2 (RS): (k1, p1) twice, k to end.

Continue as set by Rows 1 and 2 for 5 more rows. Maintaining 4 sts at center front edge in k1, p1 rib throughout, dec 1 st at end of next row (RS), then on following 8th row—35 sts rem. Work 1 WS row even.

Work Rows 1–24 of chart, beg with St 2 and ending with St 8, remembering to keep edge sts in rib.

Dec 1 st at end of next row (RS), then every following 8th row until 29 sts rem. Work 1 WS row even.

Work Rows 1–24 of chart, beg with St 2 and ending with St 8.

Dec 1 st at end of next row, then every 2nd row until 17 sts rem.

Bind off.

LEFT FRONT

Work as for Right Front, reversing shaping and beg chart with St 1, ending with St 7.

SIDE PANELS (make 2)

With MC, cast on 72 sts. Work 7 rows in St st, ending with a WS row. Dec 1 st at each end of next row and on following 8th row—68 sts rem. Work 1 WS row even.

Work Rows 1–24 of chart, beg with St 1 and ending with St 8.

Dec 1 st at each end of next row, then every following 8th row until 56 sts rem.

Work Rows 1–24 of chart, beg with St 1 and ending with St 8.

Dec 1 st at each end of next row, then next 3 RS rows, then every following row until 14 sts rem.

Bind off.

FINISHING

Weave in ends and block. Seam panels together beginning at neck edge, leaving bottom 11½ inches of seams between the front and side panels unseamed for slit openings.

Collar

With MC and RS facing and beg at right front edge, pick up and knit 92 sts around neck.

Row 1 (WS): *p2, p2tog; rep from * to end—69 sts rem.

Row 2 (RS): *k1, p1; rep from * to last st, k1.

Continue in k1, p1 rib for a total of 28 rows.

Bind off loosely in rib.

Fold collar to inside and slip-stitch bound-off edge in place. Slip-stitch or single-crochet front edges closed.

Sew snaps to front bands, evenly spaced from approximately ½ inch below the top of the slit openings to the middle of the collar. Attach buttons to RS of right front to correspond with placement of snaps.

With MC and crochet hook, work 1 row of single crochet all around bottom and slit opening edges. Weave in ends. Fringe bottom.

OHIO KNITTING MILLS

Original Design

Summer   19 73

4701 PERKINS AVENUE
CLEVELAND, O. 44103

Hippie Stashbag

It is said that you can learn everything about a woman simply based on the contents of her purse. However, one doesn't even need to glance inside the Hippie Stashbag to know its owner well.

A colorful tote meant to complement the freewheeling "wherever you go, there you are" vibe of the 1970s, Hippie Stashbag was part practicality and part fashion statement. With its wide array of ethnic patterns and a roominess that could have been inspired by the title character's grip in *Mary Poppins,* this bag was intended for the girl on the go—whether she was a chick caravanning across the country following the Grateful Dead or a liberated woman juggling an office job and motherhood.

Just imagine the plethora of paraphernalia this bag once stowed—beeswax lip balm, a dog-eared copy of *On the Road,* crinkled flyers for a weekend protest in the park, a bag of gorp, Pink Floyd ticket stubs, headbands, bubble blowers, and maybe a poncho for a cool night. This bag could hold all of a girl's needs with an of-the-moment, bohemian flair.

A timeless piece, Hippie Stashbag will do just as well holding the accoutrements of a contemporary woman.

Using extra-thick yarn, this project knits up so fast it's almost instant gratification! We line it with a simple canvas sleeve for utility, and face the strap with cotton webbing for durability and structure.

SIZE
One Size

FINISHED MEASUREMENTS
13¾ inches x 12¾ inches x 2½ inches

YARN
Cascade Yarns Magnum (100% wool; 123 yds per 250 g)
A: #9465B Burnt Orange, 1 skein
B: #0010 Ecru, 1 skein
C: #9454 Rainier Heather, 1 skein
D: #9407 Celery, 1 skein

NEEDLES
U.S. size 10.5 (6.5 mm) straight needles
Adjust needle size as needed to obtain gauge.

NOTIONS
Stitch holder
Tapestry needle
½ to 1 yd cotton canvas for lining
1 yd of 2-inch cotton webbing for strap lining
Needle and thread (and sewing machine, if desired)

GAUGE
11 sts and 14 rows = 4 inches/10 cm in St st stranded colorwork

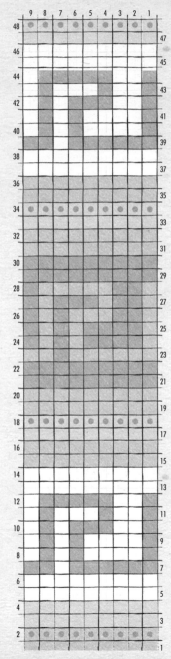

Wide Side

BASE

With A, cast on 37 sts. Work in Garter st (knit every row) for 7 rows. Bind off.

FRONT AND BACK (make 2)

With A, pick up and knit 37 sts from long side of Base. Work Rows 1–48 of Wide Side chart (opposite). Row 1 is a RS row. Bind off.

NARROW SIDE 1

With A, pick up and knit 8 sts from short side of Base. Knit 2 rows with A, ending with RS facing for next row. Then, working in St st, continue as follows: 2 rows in D; 10 rows in B; 2 rows in A; 2 rows in D; 2 rows in A; 10 rows in C; 2 rows in A; 2 rows in D; 2 rows in A; 10 rows in B; 2 rows in D.**

Place sts on holder.

NARROW SIDE 2

Work same as Narrow Side 1 to **.

Change to A and work in Garter st until strap is desired length.

Graft end of strap to 8 held sts from opposite side of bag using the Kitchener stitch.

FINISHING

Seam. Weave in ends.

Strap Facing

The strap and narrow sides of the bag are reinforced with the 2-inch-wide cotton webbing. Turn the bag inside out, and starting at the *base* edge of one of the narrow sides, carefully pin the webbing along the entire height of this side, centering it on the side panel (the webbing should be slightly narrower than the side itself). In one continuous strip, pin the webbing to the entire length of the strap and then down the other narrow side all the way to the base (see photograph 1, page 138). Cut off any excess webbing that extends beyond the base edge. Machine sew the webbing to the strap, along its entire length, 1/8 inch from each edge, taking care to adjust the foot and tensions to accommodate the thickness of the knitting and webbing. Hand sew each edge of the webbing to the side panels with a slip stitch or backstitch, then sew across the width of the webbing at the base ends and tops of the side panels. Remove all pins and turn bag right side out.

Lining

Use a tightly woven cotton fabric for your lining; we used a 7-ounce canvas, which provides a dense lining that resists puncturing by pens, knitting needles, and the like. Measure the *inside* dimensions of your bag—width, length, and height; this will determine the finished dimensions of your sewn liner. Add 1/2 inch to each measurement, and lay out a pattern matching those dimensions on your lining material. Cut out the lining as a single piece (see photograph 2, page 138), and, right sides together, machine sew the four base-to-hem seams only, leaving a 1/4-inch seam allowance. You now have a box-shaped piece with an open top. Press your seams open with an iron. Slip the lining all the way into the bag, wrong sides of the bag and lining facing, and fold under and pin in place all four sides of the top edge of the lining so it is just below the top edge of the knitted bag and the raw edge of the lining is concealed. Using a neat slip stitch all around, sew the lining to the top inside edge of the bag.

1: The cotton webbing, sewn along the wrong side of the sides and strap of the bag. 2: The lining, cut out and ready for assembly. 3: The assembled lining, ready for insertion into the knitted bag. 4: The inside edge of the finished bag, with the top edge of the lining slip-stitched into place.

PONCHOS

Woodstock everyday, everywhere

By the 1970s, the hippie movement had been partially co-opted, as persistent marketing and advertising pushed its once on-the-fringe attitudes about nonconformity, personal expression, and the like into the popular consciousness. For instance, the poncho transcended its South American roots to become a practical-to-wear and simple-to-make canvas for endless variations of patterns and palettes. In the process, its immense popularity kept OKM in the black.

OHIO KNITTING MILLS
Original Design

Fall   19 74

4701 PERKINS AVENUE
CLEVELAND, O. 44103

Earth Mother

Taking inspiration from the civil rights and antiwar movements, the women of the 1970s began to organize to promote their own equality. Although women's lib started in the previous decade, it was during the seventies that the movement gained considerable force, with key court triumphs—most notably, *Roe v. Wade*—and cultural landmarks like the publication of *Our Bodies, Ourselves* heralding the arrival of a new breed of woman. No longer did women accept simply being homemakers; they asserted themselves as important public figures as well. Out went Betty Crocker and in came Gloria Steinem.

Everyone from Erica Jong to *Ms.* magazine encouraged women to trade in domesticity and complicated undergarments for activism and flowing caftans. Women's roles became increasingly versatile, from the boardroom to the bedroom, and their voices were growing louder, particularly in the worlds of politics and environmental issues. Along with this new female consciousness, women were also encouraged to shed other "negative" aspects of the old patriarchy. Where the ladies of the 1950s were enthralled with all things synthetic and convenient, the women of the seventies were immersing themselves in the natural realm and creative social engagement—from whole foods and holistic medicine to meditation and handcrafts. Women were distancing themselves from their vacuum cleaners and pot roasts, and embracing yoga and sprouts.

The feminist movement of the 1970s also redefined feminine beauty. The liberated woman had her own aesthetic, defined by icons like Diane Keaton as the title character in *Annie Hall*, with her self-confident wardrobe combining men's accessories and hippie inspirations. Even sex symbols like Farrah Fawcett were donning the duds of women's lib—pieces just like Earth Mother.

Earth Mother captures what it meant to be an emancipated woman. Its long lines and knee-grazing length suggest stature, comfort, and confidence—a woman free from the constraints of the male idea of beauty. The dynamic pattern also has an ethnic flavor that imbues a sense of worldliness and whimsy. Whether worn at a cocktail party or for running errands, Earth Mother is a statement piece that surely announces, in Helen Reddy's words, "I am woman, hear me roar!"

This project is for the knitter who likes a challenge: knit side-to-side with stranded colorwork, short row shaping, topstitching, and crocheted edges all combined in a mid-thigh length!

SIZES
Women's S/M (L/XL)

FINISHED MEASUREMENTS
Bust 38 (45) inches
Length 34 (34½) inches (including crochet edging)

YARN
Manos del Uruguay Wool Clásica (100% wool; 137 yds per 100 g)
A: #14 Natural, 6 (7) skeins
B: #Z Straw, 4 (5) skeins
C: #37 Thrush (light brown), 4 (5) skeins
D: #G Coffee (dark brown), 4 (5) skeins

Lion Brand Lion Wool (100% wool; 158 yds per 85 g)
#820-153 Ebony, 2 skeins

NEEDLES
U.S. size 9 (5.5 mm) circular needle, 24 inches or longer
Adjust needle size as needed to obtain gauge.

NOTIONS
Tapestry needle
U.S. size I (5.5 mm) crochet hook

GAUGE
15 sts and 21½ rows = 4 inches/10 cm in St st

NOTES
All pieces are knit side-to-side. The body is given an A-line shape using short rows.

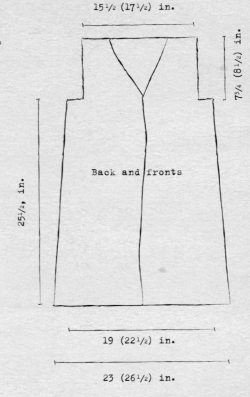

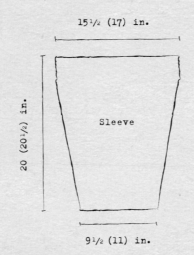

BACK

With A, cast on 96 sts. Knit 1 row (RS).

Short Row Shaping

Note: Hide wraps as you come to them.
Row 1 (WS): p18, wrap and turn.
Rows 2, 4, 6, 8: Knit.
Row 3: p36, wrap and turn.
Row 5: p54, wrap and turn.
Row 7: p72, wrap and turn.
Row 9: Purl.
  Work 1 (3) rows even in St st.
  Start working from Back chart (page 144), beg with Row 26 (31). At the end of next Row 1 (2) (WS), cast on 29 (32) sts for right armhole. Continue on these 125 (128) sts until you have 3 stripes in B, plus 2 or 3 (3 or 4) rows in A (chart Row 13 or 14 [15 or 16]) ending with a WS row. Bind off 29 (32) sts at beg of next RS row for left armhole. Continue on 96 sts following chart until you have 3 stripes in C, plus 1 or 2 (2 or 3) rows in A (chart Row 23 or 24 [29 or 30]), ending with a RS row.

Short Row Shaping

Note: Hide wraps as you come to them.
  Discontinue chart and work with A only.
Row 1 (WS): p72, wrap and turn.
Rows 2, 4, 6, 8: Knit.
Row 3: p54, wrap and turn.
Row 5: p36, wrap and turn.
Row 7: p18, wrap and turn.
Row 9: Purl.
  Bind off.

LEFT FRONT

With A, cast on 96 sts. Knit 1 row (RS).

Short Row Shaping

Note: Hide wraps as you come to them.
Row 1 (WS): p18, wrap and turn.
Rows 2, 4, 6, 8: Knit.
Row 3: p36, wrap and turn.
Row 5: p54, wrap and turn.
Row 7: p72, wrap and turn.
Row 9: Purl.
  Work 1 (3) rows even in St st.
  Start working from Front chart (page 144), beg with Row 4 (5). At the end of next Row 12 (15) (WS), cast on 29 (32) sts for armhole. Continue on these 125 (128) sts until you have completed one stripe in C (chart Row 33 [1]).

Neck Shaping

Bind off 3 sts at beg of every RS row 10 (12) times.
  Bind off rem sts.

RIGHT FRONT

With A, cast on 96 sts. Knit 1 row (RS), purl 1 row.

Short Row Shaping

Note: Hide wraps as you come to them.
Row 1 (RS): k18, wrap and turn.
Rows 2, 4, 6, 8: Purl to end.
Row 3: k36, wrap and turn.
Row 5: k54, wrap and turn.
Row 7: k72, wrap and turn.

Row 9: Knit.
  Work 0 (2) rows even in St st.
  Start working from chart, beg with Row 4 (5). At the end of next Row 11 (14) (RS), cast on 29 (32) sts for armhole. Continue on these 125 (128) sts until you have completed one stripe in C (chart Row 1 [2]).

Neck Shaping

Bind off 3 sts at beg of every WS row 10 (12) times.
  Bind off rem sts.

FIRST SLEEVE

With A, cast on 19 (21) sts. For size S/M only, p 1 row. Both sizes beg working from Back chart, beg with Row 1 (2) (RS). Cast on 7 sts at end of every following RS row until there are 75 (77) sts. When you have completed 2 stripes in D plus 1 (2) rows in A (chart Row 1 [2]), bind off 7 sts at beg of every WS row until 19 (21) sts rem. For size S/M only, work 1 row even with A. Bind off rem sts.

SECOND SLEEVE

With A, cast on 19 (21) sts. For size S/M only, p 1 row. Both sizes beg working from Front chart, beg with Row 1 (2) (RS). Cast on 7 sts at end of every following RS row until there are 75 (77) sts. When you have completed 2 stripes in C plus 1 (2) rows in A (chart Row 1 [2]), bind off 7 sts at beg of every WS row until 19 (21) sts rem. For size S/M only, work 1 row even with A. Bind off rem sts.

FINISHING

Weave in ends. Block.

With Ebony yarn, embroider in Chain st along the edges of each colored stripe.

Seam shoulders. Set sleeves into armholes. Sew side and sleeve seams.

With Ebony yarn and crochet hook, work 1 row Slip stitch, followed by 2 rows single crochet along bottom of coat.

Repeat crochet around front and neck edges, and wrists.

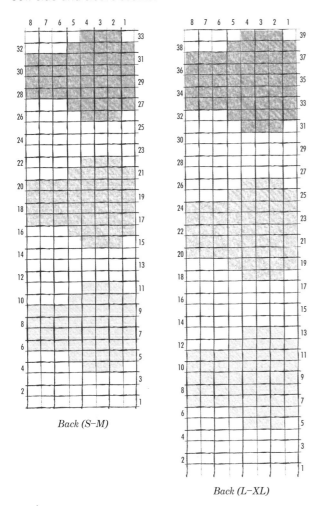

Back (S–M)

Back (L–XL)

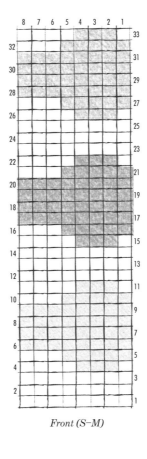

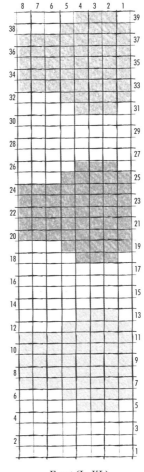

Front (S–M)

Front (L–XL)

1950s CARDIGANS

Uniform for a new casual

Everyday life for the average guy rapidly expanded in the 1950s, but the culture wasn't giving up its role defining uniforms easily. While it was commonly said that a true gentleman wouldn't go out without a jacket (and a hat), the increasingly active lifestyles that Middle America was enjoying required looser attire. The cardigan sweater moved into many gents' closets to maintain their mantle of decorum and authority, while simultaneously saying, "Relax, man." A generation later, these sweaters circled back into retro coolness.

OHIO KNITTING MILLS
Original Design

Spring ___ 19 76

4701 PERKINS AVENUE
CLEVELAND, O. 44103

Puppy Love

By the 1970s, the emerging youth culture was an omnipresent phenomenon. As a result, Ohio Knitting Mills found the majority of its business through apparel lines specifically marketed to teenagers and preteens, coyly referred to in the apparel industry as "Juniors" and "Missies." The tastes of teenagers were evident in everything from pop music to the fashion market. Whether fawning over issues of *16 Magazine,* Donny Osmond, the Jackson 5, or a Farrah Fawcett hairstyle, teen girls had staked out a large territory in mainstream culture, and OKM responded with styles made for labels with names like Girltown, Inc.; Young Naturals; Petit; and Jack Teen by Jack Winter.

Thanks to the incredible buying power of teens and their demand for affordable but totally à la mode outfits, fashion labels began producing extensive seasonal lines of mix-and-match knit separates that could be worn in the classroom as well as at the roller-skating rink. Teenagers could now visit one section of a department store for all their wardrobe needs.

The Puppy Love vest is a great example of a mid-1970s, up-to-the-minute coordinate that added attitude to any ensemble. It's a playful piece that literally spells out adolescent bliss. One can't help but think of school binders doodled with all sorts of testaments to teenage infatuation—whether for the captain of the football team or David Cassidy. The vest also speaks to the fashion trends of the times—its high-waisted cut yearns for a pair of skintight bell-bottoms, and the tailored fit and deep armholes demand nothing less than a broad butterfly-collar shirt worn underneath.

Knitting this piece will be sure to bring any gal back to her days of cutesy crushes.

The exaggerated 1-by-1 ribbed waist, steeked armholes, and stranded colorwork make this lovely project a brief but intense affair.

SIZES
To fit bust 32 (34, 36, 38, 40, 42) inches

FINISHED MEASUREMENTS
Waist 30¾ (33¼, 35¾, 38, 40, 41¾) inches
Length 17½ (17½, 18, 18, 18½, 18½) inches

YARN
Classic Elite Classic One Fifty (100% wool;
150 yds per 50 g)
MC: #7246 River's Edge, 4 (4, 5, 5,
5, 6) skeins
CC: #7201 White, 1 (1, 2, 2, 2, 2) skein

NEEDLES
U.S. size 5 (3.75 mm) circular needle,
24 inches long
U.S. size 3 (3.25 mm) circular needle,
24 inches long (body ribbing)
U.S. size 3 (3.25 mm) circular needle,
16 inches long (neck edging)
Adjust needle sizes as necessary to obtain
gauge.

NOTIONS
Stitch markers
Tapestry needle
U.S. size G (4.5 mm) crochet hook
Needle and thread

GAUGE
26 sts and 30 rows = 4 inches/10 cm in St
st with stranded colorwork pattern on larger
needles

NOTES
The Love chart (opposite) has a repeat of 20
rows and 45 sts. It is not intended to fit evenly
into the width of the vest; do not worry about
ending the front or back with a partial repeat,
as this is part of the design. However, with
each new vertical repeat (20 rows) you must
stagger the start of the chart by 15 sts, so that
the word *love* moves diagonally across the vest.
For example, with the first repeat you will begin
working the chart at St 1; with the second, at St
16; the third repeat at St 31; the fourth at St 1;
the fifth at St 16; and so on.

Vest is knit using steeks for the armholes and
neck. The vertical stripe pattern for the steek
sts is: k1 MC, k1 CC; repeat.

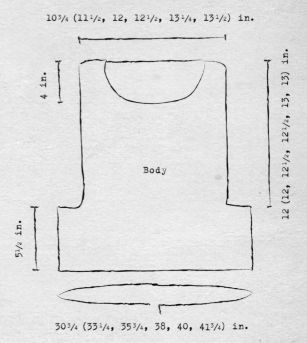

10¾ (11½, 12, 12½, 13¼, 13½) in.

4 in.

Body

5½ in.

12 (12, 12¼, 12½, 13, 13) in.

30¾ (33¼, 35¾, 38, 40, 41¾) in.

BODY

With smaller 24-inch needle and MC, cast on 200 (216, 232, 248, 260, 272) sts. Place marker and join to work in the round. Work k1, p1 rib for 5½ inches. On last rnd, place a second marker at the halfway point of the rnd, after 100 (108, 116, 124, 130, 136) sts.

Armhole Steeks

Next rnd: Rib to 15 (17, 19, 21, 22, 24) sts before second marker, bind off 30 (34, 38, 42, 44, 48) sts, removing the second marker; continue rib to 15 (17, 19, 21, 22, 24) sts before beg-of-rnd marker, bind off 30 (34, 38, 42, 44, 48) sts, removing the marker—70 (74, 78, 82, 86, 88) sts rem each side.

Change to larger needle.

Next rnd: Knit to bound-off sts, cast on 7 sts for steek, k to second set of bound-off sts, cast on 7 sts for steek, pm for new beg of rnd.

Begin Colorwork

Rnd 1: Work Rnd 1 of Love chart (right) to steek sts, work steek sts in vertical stripe patt (see Notes), work Rnd 1 of chart to second set of steek sts, work steek sts in vertical stripe patt.

Continue to work in patt as established until armholes measure 8 (8, 8½, 8½, 9, 9) inches.

Neck Steek

Next rnd (front): Work 14 (15, 16, 17, 18, 19) sts in patt, bind off center 42 (44, 46, 48, 50, 50) sts for front neck, work 14 (15, 16, 17, 18, 19) sts in patt. **(Back):** work in patt to end.

Next rnd: Work to bound-off sts, cast on 7 sts for steek, work in patt to end.

Next rnd: Work to neck steek sts, work steek sts in vertical stripe patt, work in patt to end.

Next rnd: Work to 3 sts before neck steek sts, k2tog, k1, work steek sts in vertical stripe patt, k1, ssk, work in patt to end.

Rep the last 2 rnds twice more—11 (12, 13, 14, 15, 16) sts rem on each side of front neck (exclusive of steeks).

Work even in patt as established until vest measures 17½ (17½, 18, 18, 18½, 18½) inches.

Bind off all sts.

FINISHING

Sew and cut steek sts (see page 153).

Seam shoulders.

Neckband

With 16-inch needle and MC, beg at left shoulder with RS facing, pick up and knit 1 st in each bound-off st and 2 sts for every 3 rows around neckline, pm and join for working in the round. Adjust st count as necessary to achieve a multiple of 2 sts. Work k1, p1 rib for 1 inch. Bind off in rib. Tack steek sts down on inside.

Armbands

On armholes, turn cut steek edges to inside and steam to hold in place. With crochet hook and MC, work 1 rnd of single crochet around armhole edges, *working through both layers of fabric* (the face of the vest and the turned-under steeks).

Weave in ends. Block. Block bottom ribbing aggressively to bring it out to the correct width.

Make sure armholes are secure, then trim steeks to neaten.

LABELS

When every city had its own look

Until its current twenty-first-century incarnation, Ohio Knitting Mills was strictly a contract manufacturer. It produced goods for many designers and retailers across the country, and each of these customers had its own label, which was sewn into each finished garment by the mill. These labels could be geographic, typographic, and even illustrative. Sophisticated or naïve, elegant or playful, they were tiny calling cards sewn into every piece.

Candyknit
38
SOFT AND SWEET...U NEXT TO YOU
RN 30609

Penney's
42
HAND WASHABLE
100% WOOL   WPL 11935

CAMPUS
CASUALS
OF CALIFORNIA

Royal Choice
100% ORLON

White Stag
SKI TOGS
WHITE STAG MFG. CO. PORTLAND, OREGON

Churchill
100%
WOOL

LUVLEE
Lady®

SPORTSWEAR
by
FLAMINGO
S

Mimi Martin
MIMI MARTIN MILLS
a California Creation

100% Wool R.L.D.
by
Ralph
R. L. DAVIS MFG. CO.

THIS IS A
BENRUB
COPYRIGHT 1926
GUARANTEED
100% ALL WOOL
SWEATER

ALL WOOL
Rugby
Knitting
BUFFALO, N.Y. MILLS
It for All Good Sports

100% WOOL
STYLED BY
Stoneleigh
REG. U.S. PAT. OFF.
New York
L. D. LIVINGSTON & SONS

Side KICKS

Peaksdale
100% ALL WOOL

STYLED by Oxford Hall
Millman SPORTSWEAR

JackTeen
BY JACK WINTER

Zado of CALIFORNIA

Brittony
Brand
CHICAGO

BAN-LON
Quality Garment
Ban-Lon®
BY
Revere®
100% DUPONT ANTRON NYLON

GLOSSARY OF KNITTING TECHNIQUES

STEEKING

Steeking is a method of preparing knitting so that the fabric may be cut (in order to form armholes or open the front of a cardigan) without causing the sweater to unravel or interrupting any pattern motifs. It is commonly used in stranded colorwork, since it allows the knitting to proceed in the round without needing to split the work and purl back in pattern.

To Set Up a Steek

At the point where you intend to cut the armholes or neckline, bind off the number of stitches directed by the pattern. These stitches will form the base of the armhole or neckline.

When on the next round you come to the gap created by the bound-off stitches, cast on 5–7 new stitches (these are the cutting stitches) and continue knitting in the round.

Work these extra stitches in a checkered or vertically striped pattern (*1 stitch color A, 1 stitch color B; repeat from*).

To Secure and Cut a Steek

Find the center stitch of the steek. Use contrasting yarn threaded on a tapestry needle to baste directly down the center of the steek. With a sewing machine and regular thread, sew a line of straight stitching on either side of the basting. Cut on the basted line.

To Finish a Steek

Pick up stitches for a ribbed or hemmed edge as directed in the pattern, working in the first column of stitches on the garment proper and leaving the steek free. When edging is complete, fold the steek flap to the inside of the work and steam-press in place. If desired, use needle and thread and herringbone or catch-stitch to tack the facing in place. (If using 100% wool, this may not be needed, because the fabric will adhere to itself with washing and wear.)

SHORT ROW SHAPING (WRAP AND TURN)

Short rows are simply incomplete rows of knitting; you stop knitting before the end of the row, turn the work, and purl back. Short rows allow you to make one part of your knitting taller (or if knitting side-to-side, wider) than the rest. In order to hide the small hole that is produced when you reverse direction midrow, you wrap the working yarn around the last stitch before turning. This leaves a bit of extra yarn that, when picked up and knit together with the wrapped stitch, disguises the hole.

To Wrap and Turn on a Knit Row

Slip the next stitch purlwise with yarn in back, bring yarn to front of work between needles, return slipped stitch to left needle without twisting it, turn work.

To Wrap and Turn on a Purl Row

Slip the next stitch purlwise with yarn in back, bring yarn to back of work between needles, return slipped stitch to left needle without twisting it, turn work.

When you come to a wrapped stitch on a subsequent knit row, hide the wrap by inserting the right needle into the wrap as if to knit it, then into the wrapped stitch, and knitting the two together. (For wraps on the purl side of the work, you will need to insert the right needle through the wrap as if to purl from *behind* the stitch, then into the wrapped stitch, and purl the two together.) If you've hidden the wrap correctly, the right side of the work will look normal, and the wrong side will have a small extra loop of yarn on the surface.

INTARSIA

Intarsia is a method of working a design in different colors. It is best suited to patterns with large areas of a single color. To work intarsia, follow the applicable chart (reading from bottom to top, right to left on right-side rows, left to right on wrong-side rows), working with one color at a time, and a separate skein or bobbin for each section. When you drop one color to pick up the next, be sure to pick up the new color from *underneath* the old, so that the two yarns are twisted together at the join.

STRANDED COLORWORK

Stranded colorwork is a method of working a design in different colors. It is best suited to smaller, repeating patterns. To work stranded colorwork, follow the applicable chart (reading from bottom to top, right to left on right-side rows, left to right on wrong-side rows), working with each color as appropriate, and carrying the color not in use loosely behind the work ("stranding" or "floats"). It is very important to keep the stranding loose, otherwise the fabric will be tight and puckered.

THREE-NEEDLE BIND OFF

The three-needle bind off is used to join two sets of live stitches, as at the shoulder of a sweater. Have each set of stitches to be joined on a separate needle. Hold the two needles together, parallel, with right sides of the work facing each other. Insert the tip of a third needle into the first stitch on the front needle, then the first stitch on the back needle, and knit the two stitches together. *Insert the tip of the third needle into the next stitch on the front needle, then the next stitch on the back needle, and knit the two stitches together. Pass the first stitch on the right needle over the second to bind off. Repeat from * until all required stitches are bound off.

APPLIED I-CORD

Applied I-cord gives a neat, round finish to edges. You will need two double-pointed needles to create it. The right side of the garment should be facing you as you work.

Cast on 4 sts. *K3. Slip the last stitch, use the tip of the right needle to pick up 1 stitch from the garment edge, pass the slipped stitch over the picked-up stitch. Slide all 4 sts back to the other end of the needle. Bring the yarn *firmly* across the back of the work. Repeat from *.

When applying I-cord to a stockinette fabric, a pickup ratio of 3 sts for every 4 rows along the garment edge is usually correct. If the cord ripples, try picking up only 2 sts for every 3 rows.

PROVISIONAL CAST-ON

A provisional cast-on is one that can be easily taken out later, revealing a row of live stitches. There are several methods; the one we suggest here requires a crochet hook and waste yarn of roughly the same weight as your main yarn.

With waste yarn, crochet a chain of the required number of cast-on sts plus a few extra. Fasten off. Put a knot in the yarn tail so you know which end to pull later.

With knitting needle and main color, pick up 1 st in each of the "bumps" (loops) on the back of the crochet chain until you have the correct number.

When it's time to remove the provisional cast-on, undo the fastened-off end and pull the tail to unravel the starting chain.

ACKNOWLEDGMENTS

Like the creations of Ohio Knitting Mills itself, this book is a collaborative effort on behalf of many talented people. My deepest thanks go to my co-author, Denise Grollmus, who was an inspiring companion on this trip through America's cultural soul. A number of extremely able professional knitters tackled the complex challenges of re-creating fifty-year-old machine-knit sweaters into the projects that glow throughout these pages: Galina Carroll, Sarah James, Sue Jaloweic, Kim Craig, Laura Huber, and Hannah Tatar. In addition to knitting some of the sweaters, Alexandra Virgiel wrote many of the knitting patterns and edited all of them. Shannon Okey also provided guidance and direction. Becca Del Pizza, Maxwell Stern, and Lucy Tatar were our terrific interns with fiber and film, and Peter Posen Jr. was my studiomate and graphics consultant through much of the project. Peter Woodworth, Marc Frisch, and Agnes Harichovsky enthusiastically shared their many memories and stories of the mill and Cleveland's garment industry past.

I have had the good fortune to work with the marvelous folks at my publisher, the so aptly named Artisan. Susan Baldaserini crafted the beautiful design of the book with art direction from Jan Derevjanik, while Ingrid Abramovich provided her eloquent editorial eye, and Trent Duffy shepherded the whole project to completion with endless patience and good-natured guidance. Trent also arranged for the important contributions of a squad of knitter/editors, including Keonaona Peterson and Andrea Molitor: I'm grateful to them and to Kristin Nicolas, who helped me out with the embroidery. And my generous gratitude goes to Caroline Greeven, who had the original vision for this book, persuaded me to attempt it, and brought this group together. Anna Wolf photographed the beautiful shots of the finished projects and Lauri Eisenberg styled them with such panache. Barton Quillen at Czech Kolektiv contributed the fabulous mid-century Czech furnishings that appear in many of the shots. We have had the great generosity of Cascade Yarns, Fairmount Fibers, and Classic Elite Yarns in providing us with numerous beautiful yarns to work with; I heartily urge other knitters to seek them out.

I'm very appreciative of the many people around the world who have supported and inspired me in evolving Ohio Knitting Mills. Several deserve exceptional praise: Jerry Murphy and Elie and Zev Weiss showed extraordinary support and faith in me as I began this venture, which allowed OKM to open its Brooklyn storefront/showroom, and Nora Murphy and Celene Ryan provided caring and cheerful stewardship of this outpost as our community of customers grew. Jean Sebastian Sardo and Andrea Esposito opened their hearts and home to me and welcomed me into their family so that I might coexist in two different cities when the venture required. And I've been so very lucky to have the ongoing friendship, camaraderie, and couchette of my Buckeye brother in Brooklyn, Phil Smrek.

Infinite love to Terre Maher, my infinitely patient partner and the mother of our amazing girls. Finally, the greatest thanks and respect of all must go to the Stone-Rand family, who are, after all, the true geniuses who created so much of what this book celebrates, and who have entrusted me to preserve their family legacy.

—STEVEN TATAR

Cleveland sculptor **Steven Tatar** was hunting for scrap metal when he stumbled upon the now-shuttered Ohio Knitting Mills. He bought the company's sweater archive and opened Ohio Knitting Mills, a stylish Brooklyn storefront, where for two years he sold vintage knits that had never been worn. He now sells limited-edition sweaters on his Web site, www .OhioKnittingMills.com.

Denise Grollmus is a nonfiction writer who has covered everything from binge-drinking Amish girls to mercenary boxers. Her work has appeared in such places as *The Best American Crime Writing 2006, Waxpoetics, Spin,* the *Akron Beacon Journal, Cleveland Free Times,* and *Cleveland Scene.* She lives in Akron, Ohio.

ILLUSTRATION CREDITS

The contemporary fashion photographs for the twenty-six projects in the book are by Anna Wolf. All other photographs and illustrations are provided by Steven Tatar, unless listed below. The authors and the publisher thank the following for permission to use their photographs or illustrations in this book.